CREATED TO RULE
TOGETHER

Copyright © 2007 Frances Pike

Printed in the United States of America

Published by:
Mall Publishing
641 Homewood Avenue
Highland Park, Illinois 60035
877.203.2453

Cover and text design by Marlon Villadiego.

All Scriptures are from the New King James Version unless otherwise noted.

All rights reserved. No part of this book may be reproduced or transmitted in any form or by any means, graphic, electronic, or mechanical, including photocopying, recording, taping, or by any information storage or retrieval system, without the permission in writing from the publisher.

ISBN: 1-934165-30-1

For licensing / copyright information,
for additional copies or for use in specialized settings contact:

SpiritLife Ministries
3519 NW 41 St
Oklahoma City, OK 73112
splmin@aol.com

INTRODUCTION BY J. LEE GRADY

CREATED TO RULE
TOGETHER

A CALL FOR GENDER BALANCED LEADERSHIP

FRANCES PIKE

HIGHLAND PARK, ILLINOIS

DEDICATION

To my Mother, Beulah Thornton

Who co-labored with my father, Rev. Laddie
Thornton [1920-2001], in pastoral ministry.

To this generation of men and women who
will rise up to rule together in the earth.

TABLE OF CONTENTS

PREFACE

Out of life experiences and revelation from God, Frances received a mandate to write *Created to Rule Together: A Call to Gender Balanced Leadership*. From our leadership assignments and ministry together, we began to recognize the value of each other's contribution to balanced leadership and ruling together. Each gender brings a God-given grace to the leadership team. Without a gender balance, leadership is tilted or skewed with a vital dimension missing. But together, with each accepting the other, God's design for leadership and ruling is fulfilled.

This book is not about husband and wife relationships, but the home is the laboratory for testing Christian leadership. For over forty years, Frances and I have spent our lives growing in a greater understanding of each other. It really began when we taught a marriage and family course in an institution I served. Through this course, we came to realize by the profile tests taken during this time what we already knew – we were vastly different. So much that we wondered why God had led us together. From this discovery, we pledged to grow in our understanding of each other.

As we raised our wonderful God-given children, Janese and Jay, we tried to follow the roles of father and mother as taught in all the textbooks we used in the marriage and family courses. However, we found they were constricting and artificial as we tried to apply them. They did not fit us. The same was true of leadership roles we embraced. Both of us tried to follow the advice of various leadership gurus, but found something missing. With our one flesh commitment of marriage, little or no mention was made of the gender contribution each makes to the leadership equation. The pathway of Frances' career took many turns as a wife and mother, public school teacher, pastor's wife, Bible teacher, and a leader of women's prayer groups including a leading contribution to the city-wide prayer movement in Oklahoma City. In all of these roles, my wisdom and input was sought and received. Whenever she went overseas to minister, my blessing, encouragement, and prayers partnered in her ministry, even though I was not physically present. In my role as dean of an undergraduate and now a graduate program, her input, wisdom and counsel has been vital to my success. We did not find any instructional manuals for gender-balanced leadership but by God's grace discovered this great truth. From the crucible of these life experiences and a thorough search of scriptures, accompanied by solid research of the current literature, there emerged an understanding of gender-balanced and co-equal leadership.

But this truth is not limited to a husband and wife relationship. Truth is universal and applies to all leadership assignments. The valuable contribution of each gender brings a balance to the leadership process, resulting in a greater effectiveness. Frances' book, *Created to Rule Together: a Call to Gender Balanced Leadership,* will encourage all to examine this important dimension of leadership.

Dr. Garnet E. Pike, Dean
Graduate School
Southwestern Christian University
Bethany, Oklahoma

ACKNOWLEDGEMENTS

I honor my father, Laddie Thornton, who served as a pastor for over 30 years. He instilled biblical convictions in me and encouraged me to attempt anything for God.

My husband, Garnet Pike, has been my teacher and trainer. I would not be who I am today had God not used Garnet to refine me. He has lived the patience and longsuffering of God before me and our children. He has been a constant support to me in this assignment.

I am honored that Lee Grady, Editor of *Charisma,* would write the Introduction to this book. He has authored two books related to the subject of this book. More importantly he is practicing what he preaches. He is standing with women in leadership by speaking in conferences led by women and being a part of a network led by a woman.

I am deeply grateful to Angela Davis for her professional expertise in editing and preparing the manuscript for publication. Without her help, this book would not have been published.

There have been some key male leaders in my life who have encouraged me in this assignment: My thanks to Dr. J. Robert Clinton, Dr. Sam Chand, Dr. C. Peter Wagner and Dr. Chuck Pierce for your encouragement.

My thanks to Pastor Barbara Yoder for her listening ear and input to the manuscript.

The professional opinion of Carolyn DeLeon, who serves as Vice President of Human Resources for a major hospital, was most insightful.

Without committed intercessors I would have become weary. Thanks to each one of you for your prayers and encouragement—Billie

Boatwright, Kathy Shelley, Sharon Compton, Linda Smith, Dana Miller, Rita Terry, Lisa Lyons, Marian Duvall, Diana Lookabaugh, JoAnne Bailey.

INTRODUCTION

A BIBLICAL MANDATE
FOR GENDER PARTNERSHIP
BY J. LEE GRADY

The Bible contains numerous examples of godly women who held positions of spiritual authority and influence. Eve, the first woman, was commissioned by God to "subdue the earth" alongside her husband. Sarah, the true "mother of our faith," believed with Abraham for the promised Isaac and inherited the promised land of Canaan. Miriam led Israel with her brothers Moses and Aaron. Deborah, as the appointed prophet, ruled her nation as a judge and rallied the people to victory over enemy armies. Huldah, a contemporary of the prophet Jeremiah, counseled the court of Josiah and foretold the coming judgments on Israel. And Esther, as queen in the Persian court, used her authority to unravel Haman's genocidal plot against the Jews.

In the New Testament, we find an equal number of women who served in positions of spiritual authority. The apostle Paul said of Phoebe the deacon: "I commend to you our sister," and endorsed her as an extension of his own ecclesiastical authority. He also applauded Junia, a female apostle who spent time in prison for her faith. (Some Bible scholars insist that her name is "Junias" and that she was actually a man, but this interpretation did not begin to circulate until the 1300s. A careful study of early biblical texts and names used in the First Century point us to the conclusion that Junia was in fact a powerful Christian woman who impacted the Roman world with the gospel.)

In the book of Acts we are introduced to the woman Priscilla, a gifted Bible teacher who ministered in partnership with her husband, Aquilla. Together these two launched the man Apollos into apostleship. We also read about Euodia, Syntyche, Nympha and the four daughters of Philip—all women who served either as prophets, pastors or church planters in the first century.

Yet despite the clear record of Scripture, modern evangelicals tend to ignore these women even while championing a so-called literal approach to the Bible. The truth is these literalists are actually twisting Scripture. They do not accept what the Bible says. Instead, when the Bible endorses women in leadership positions, they conveniently ignore these references—and might as well snip them out of the Scriptures. Then they claim that Paul's words in I Timothy 2:12 (in which Paul warns Timothy not to allow certain women to teach heresy) automatically overrule all the rest of Scripture and create a binding, universal mandate that prevents all women for all time from assuming any positions of church authority.

But is this true? Did the Apostle Paul's words to Timothy create an ironclad prohibition against women in leadership, as many fundamentalist and evangelical Christians insist?

The "no women in authority" rule is quite curious, since it can only be derived from a surface reading of the I Timothy passage ("But I do not allow a woman to teach or to exercise authority over a man, but to remain quiet," NASB.) The King James Version is a bit clearer, translating "exercise authority" as "*usurp* authority" (emphasis added), a more accurate rendering of the Greek text. Actually, there is no word in the English language to accurately translate *authentein*, although "usurp" is close enough. The Greek verb denotes a violent act with almost murderous connotations.

Scholars who read this passage in harmony with the rest of the Bible (which already allows for trained, gifted women in authority) have concluded that Paul obviously was dealing with a problematic situation in the Ephesian church. Most likely he was clamping down on a particular woman, or a group of women, who were teaching Gnostic heresies that suggested that Eve was created before Adam and therefore was superior to him. The cult of Diana, which operated in Ephesus at that time and was often led by pagan priestesses, also blended worship of the goddess with sexual immorality. Paul was right to clamp down on this brand of false teaching when it invaded the early church—and his solution was not only to muzzle the women involved but to demand that they submit "in silence" to the teaching of proper doctrine.

What is most curious about the Timothy passage is that Paul, while warning his young disciple about the dangers of these female heretics, praises Timothy's own mother and grandmother for laying spiritual foundations in his life. Paul said to his young disciple: "For I am mindful of the sincere faith within you, which first dwelt in your grandmother Lois and your mother Eunice, and I am sure that it is in you as well" (2 Tim. 1:5).

Was Paul being schizophrenic here? On one hand he tells women teachers to be quiet, while on the other hand he praises them for their influence on Timothy. The words of Paul in this epistle create some curious tensions and cause us to ask probing questions that are still debated in the church today.

Does I Timothy 2:12 mean women are allowed to teach in the home but not in the church? Are women allowed to teach children but not adults? Are women capable of understanding doctrine well enough to impart it to youngsters or illiterate women but not mature enough or capable enough to impart it to men? Does the fact that Paul seems to crack down on women teachers in Ephesus mean that he did not believe women could ever teach or lead? If so, why did he so heartily endorse Priscilla, Phoebe, Euodia, Syntyche and Junia?

THE MISSING DYNAMIC: SPIRITUAL MOTHERS

We can find the answer to these questions by exploring what the Bible says about motherly authority. The Scriptures are replete with references to the influence of a woman over her own children. In Proverbs, a son is warned not to abandon the instruction of his mother. Throughout Scripture parents are challenged as couples to use discipline, instruction, exhortation and the rod of correction to train their youngsters. And in the New Testament, women whose husbands are not even believers are told that they possess priestly authority to influence their families for righteousness (see I Peter 3:1-3).

We also see that in the New Testament church, older women who were godly examples to a congregation were often set apart to serve in a special capacity. The word for "older women" in Titus 2:3 is the word *presbytera*, from which we derive the word presbytery, or elders' council. In the early church, those who had accumulated wisdom and godly character were designated as elders so that they could "teach what is good" (Titus 2:3b). And the early church had women who were viewed as elders because they were such good examples to the flock.

God never intended only men to nurture the church. Just as he gave each child two parents—a mother and a father—He desires spiritual mothers and fathers to instruct and edify God's people. Yet in many tradition-bound churches today—where wrongheaded views of gender are imposed and women are restricted—there is no room for spiritual mothers. Somehow we have twisted the Bible to suggest that it is never appropriate for a woman to teach or influence a man. Therefore we have become a motherless people. And thus, tragically, we have fewer Timothys emerging.

In the book of Acts, we see a beautiful example of a spiritual mother in the woman Priscilla, who instructed the man Apollos and launched him into apostolic ministry (see Acts 18:24-28). Why is this scene in the Bible? Priscilla is mentioned four times in the Scriptures, and in three of those places her name is mentioned first. Many scholars believe that this is because she was the more prominent public figure due to her visible teaching ministry.

That occurred in New Testament times. Yet in many churches today, because we wrongly assume that Paul did not allow women in the pulpit or in leadership roles, we have forbidden spiritual mothers to function. They are not allowed to teach, bring correction, model godliness or impart revelation. And we are weaker for it.

Another excellent biblical picture of a spiritual mother can be found in Judges 4, in the story of Deborah and the man Barak, who was the leader of Israel's armies. We are told that Barak advised Deborah that he would not go into battle without her. He said: "If you will go with me I will go; but if you will not go with me, I will not go" (Judges 4:6).

Chauvinists who read their biases into this passage assume that Barak must have been some sort of "mama's boy" because he was afraid to fight without a woman by his side. That is actually a twisted interpretation of this verse, since we know from reading Hebrews 11:32 that Barak is honored as a man of remarkable faith. Actually, his request to have Deborah by his side was an act of courage—because he knew she was God's prophet and he wanted access to her godly counsel during the battle with the Canaanites.

It would have been the height of stupidity for Barak to go into battle without this woman, since she was God's designated leader for that season in Israel's history. His decision to submit to her leadership also opened the door for another woman, Jael, to strike the final blow to the enemy's head.

This should show us today that if we deny the influence of spiritual mothers, we also will forfeit some strategic victories. So many leaders in the church today think they are doing God's will by appointing only men to pastoral positions, elder boards, deacons' councils and church leadership posts. This is actually nothing more than reliance on the arm of the flesh. God has placed His spiritual gifts in every member of the body of Christ, irrespective of race, class or gender. To deny qualified women their place at the table is to limit the reach of God's grace and favor. And to deny spiritual mothers their role is to limit spiritual reproduction.

It is time for the church today to fling open the doors and allow our spiritual mothers to take their places on the front lines. We need their wisdom, their passion, their supernatural giftings, their instruction and their correction. Only when they are positioned alongside the men of the church will we truly be able to see the manifest power and presence of God released fully in our midst.

1

CREATED TOGETHER

> "So God created man in His own image;
> in the image of God He created him;
> male and female He created them"
> (Gen. 1:27).

What an awesome truth! God, the Creator of all things, created you in His image. We need to stop and ponder that reality. You were not an accident. You are not a clone. You are a unique creation of God. You are created male or female in His image for His purposes. Both men and women are created in His image.

Understanding the original language of Genesis 1:27 gives us greater insight into God's creation. The word for "man" in this verse in the Hebrew text is "adam". In the creation account, "man" is intended to be understood as "mankind" or "humanity" which would include both the male and the female. Strong's Dictionary defines "adam" as a human being (an individual or the species, mankind, etc.)[1] Vine's Expository Dictionary agrees: Adam is also used in reference to any given man or to anyone male or female.[2]

Genesis chapter five verses one and two further confirm this understanding of creation. "This is the book of the genealogy of Adam. In the day that God created man, He made him in the likeness of God. He created them male and female, and blessed

them and called them Mankind in the day they were created".
Understanding the creation of Adam as humankind is essential.
Otherwise, we would have to assume that Eve was not put out of
the Garden of Eden. Genesis 3:24 says, "So He drove out the man"
includes woman as well. God's original intent in creating mankind
was not complete without the creation of the female species of
mankind. Both male and female were created in the image of God.

ROLE VS IDENTITY

Most of my life I believed that God created the male species
in His image and female was created in the image of man. Though I
never said it, that was the reality of what I lived. I came face-to-face
with that reality after I had been married several years and was active
in ministry with my husband. He received an invitation to be part of
a prophetic ministry team for a conference. I clearly recognized that
I was not included, but he insisted that I go with him as I had the
stronger prophetic gift. Only at his insistence did I go to the orientation.
I sat beside my husband quite uncomfortably. Everyone was asked
to introduce themselves. My husband introduced himself. And then I
said, "I am his spouse, Frances." When introductions were completed,
the leader said that only those who received a specific invitation to the
meeting should attend. After hearing that statement, I picked up my
belongings and left. What happened next greatly impacted my life. I
sensed someone behind me and heard him say, "You are more than a
spouse." I turned and saw no one. I was a bit shaken and went straight
to our hotel room. When my husband came in, I asked him if anyone
followed me out. He said, "No, you were the only one who left." I

can not explain what happened, but I know God used it to help me understand that my identity is not determined by my role.

We can become confused in our identity and destiny by thinking we are the role or position we serve. Roles and positions determined by people are temporary. You may have trusted God to position you, but you chose to accept or reject it. Our gender is determined by God. It is part of your sovereign identity and destiny. Accept yourself as created by God as male or female. There is no shame in the creation of God, only sin brings shame.

My father desired a boy as his firstborn child. When God gave him a girl, he often said, "She should have been a boy." Though he was innocent in his comment, subconsciously it affected me. For years I tried to prove I could be as good as any boy at anything. In my adult years, I faced this lie, "It is a shame to be a woman." The Holy Spirit brought the truth to me. "It is good that God made you a woman." Accepting my sovereign identity as a female was a liberating experience for me. I forgave my father and repented to God for not accepting His wisdom in creating me as woman.

We can have roots of bitterness imbedded in our souls against God for His sovereign design in our lives. Accepting our gender, nationality or place of birth will free us from bitter roots against God. God gave you a unique DNA. As a friend of mine says, "After God created you, He said, 'I will never do that again!'" Begin to believe that God's creation is good.

MARITAL STATUS MISCONCEPTION

Second, your marital status does not determine your destiny. History records many examples of women who became widows and went on to fulfill their destiny. A biblical example is Anna, the prophetess of Jesus birth. Luke tells us that she served in the temple as a widow of eighty-four years. She lived to recognize and proclaim the One she had been destined to see – Jesus Christ (Luke 2:36-38). Bishop Margaret Benson-Idahusa is a modern day example of a widow who became presiding bishop of one of the largest Pentecostal churches in Africa, the Church of God Mission International. There are also countless single women who have fulfilled the will of God for their lives.

Phoebe is a New Testament woman whom Paul commends in Romans 16. It is not clearly known if she was a widow or an unmarried woman. She obviously was an effective leader. Paul trusted her with his own letter (no carbon copy) to carry over the long and dangerous journey to Rome. The church is told to receive her. The word is *prosdechomai*, "to receive to one's self, to give access to one's self, to receive into intercourse and companionship." Paul exhorts the Roman saints to receive Phoebe "in the Lord". In Weust Word Studies, Denney remarks, "No mere reception of Phoebe into their houses satisfies this — their Christian life was to be open for her to share in it; she was no alien to be debarred from spiritual intimacy."[3]

Paul further describes Phoebe as "for she hath been a succourer of many, and of myself also." The word for succourer is *prostates* and Thayer's Lexicon description is:

a. properly, a woman set over others

b. a female guardian, protectress, patroness, caring for the affairs of others and aiding them with her resources[4]

Paul's recommendation of her was as a personal aid to him. Phoebe is an example of a single woman partnering with a New Testament apostle in ministry. We must recognize the importance of single women being given opportunity to serve God as equal recipients of the grace of God. We are all made in His image.

When God said, "Let us make man in our image," the word "make" has a secondary meaning: "to appoint". Male and female are appointed or sealed with the image of God. In the New Testament, Jesus asked the disciples whose image was on the coin. They acknowledged it was Caesar's image. Jesus replied, "Render to Caesar what is Caesar's and to God what is His" (Matt. 22:18-22). So the image determined the ownership of the coin. Mankind, both male and female, was stamped with the image of God from the beginning. "Image is a reflection of something. It is defined figuratively as an illusion, resemblance."[5]

God's image obviously does not consist in man's body which was formed from earthly matter, but in his spiritual, intellectual, moral likeness of God from whom his animating breath came.[6] Since God created male and female in His image as spiritual beings, we relate to Him as a spirit being. John declares clearly, "God is Spirit, and those who worship Him must worship in spirit and truth" (John 4:24). It is the spiritual aspect of humankind that gives us the ability and privilege of communion with God. All the plants and creatures had the ability to reproduce life and were created "after their own kind".

Only humankind was created not after their kind, but in the image of God—spirit beings.

We understand that God is spirit; therefore, He has no race or sex. God as spirit is imaged in human kind –all races and both sexes. God is not white male or black female. He is not Asian or Latino. He is Spirit and indwells human beings. As humans created in His image, we are spirit beings with the potential of being indwelt by God, the Holy Spirit. When we choose to accept Jesus and are born of the spirit, we are then indwelt by God who is spirit. We are in Christ who is the perfect image of God and through Him, we are being perfected in our reflection of God. "And have clothed yourselves with the new [spiritual self], which is [ever in the process of being] renewed and remolded into [fuller and more perfect knowledge upon] knowledge after the image (the likeness) of Him Who created it. [Gen. 1:26.]" (Col. 3:10, AMP).

Re-creation is essential because Adam and Eve's disobedience violated God's image and their relationship with Him. Actually, we bear the image of Adam since we are descendants of our first parents. The Last Adam, Jesus, restores the image of God in us. We become partakers of His image in our rebirth. Only relationship with God through faith in Jesus stamps us as children of God.

Our sexual identity does not determine the image of God in us. Carl Henry says, "The God of the Bible is a sexless God. When Scripture speaks of God as 'he' the pronoun is primarily personal (generic) rather than masculine (specific); it emphasizes God's personality…in contrast to impersonal entities."[7] The generic term "man" includes woman. In the narrative of the creation (Gen. 1:26-27), Adam is a collective term for mankind. It may signify human being, male or female, or humanity entirely.[8]

When God created Adam and Eve, He was creating humankind, both male and female, equal in the image of God. We are sealed with His image as spirit beings and are in the process of being conformed to that image (Rom. 8:26). We are being conformed to the image of God. Our character or nature should mirror God's nature. This nature has nothing to do with sexuality. It is a conforming of our character to God's character. Both men and women are in the process of becoming more God-like. Our old nature, corrupted by sin, is dying daily so the new nature is manifested in our lives. "This concrete essence of the divine likeness was shattered by sin; it is only through Christ, the brightness of the glory of God and the expression of His essence (Heb. 1:3) that our nature is transformed into the image of God again" (Col. 3:10; Eph. 4:24).[9]

Another aspect of the image of God is the fact that God is one and yet three. He said, "Let Us make man in Our image." God being plural as the trinity, yet one, was part of the image of God for mankind. Male and female are two of the same one. God did not create female from the ground. Instead, God took one and made two. She was "bone of my bone, flesh of my flesh" according to Adam. Mankind as male and female was to reflect the plurality of God as trinity. "Let us make man. The three persons of the Trinity, Father, Son, and Holy Ghost, consult about it and concur in it, because man, when he was made, was to be dedicated and devoted to Father, Son and Holy Ghost."[10] "The interrelationship between male and female symbolizes the interrelationship within God. There is no possibility, according to these verses, that Adam, the male, could by himself reflect the nature of God. Neither is it possible for Adam, the female, by herself to reflect God's nature."[11]

We teach and preach unity of the Body of Christ yet often we have not made it to level one – the unity of genders which God intended from the beginning. Accepting one another as equal members of the Body of Christ will begin to restore the glory of God. Romans says clearly, "May the God who gives endurance and encouragement give you a spirit of unity among yourselves as you follow Christ Jesus, so that with one heart and mouth you may glorify the God and Father of our Lord Jesus Christ. Accept one another, then just as Christ accepted you in order to bring praise to God" (Rom. 15:5-8, NIV). When men and women come together in full acceptance of one another God is glorified.

Adam and Eve shared open, unashamed communion or unity with God and each other in Genesis 1 and 2. Sin broke that communion and put male and female in a relationship of guilt and shame. The image of God in them became distorted. Through history we can see that the image of God continues to be distorted by the way in which men and women relate to one another. In *Why Not Women?*, David Hamilton has an entire chapter on "Distorting the Image". He documents the effects of Greek philosophy on Jewish rabbis.

> "Most rabbis would not think of teaching the Torah to a woman. Rabbis such as Gamaliel, Paul's mentor, who taught his daughter, were the rare exception...The rabbis taught that to be in right relationship with God, you had to observe the Law He gave Moses at Sinai. Yet that law was binding only on free adult males. Therefore, no children, no slaves, and no women could serve God fully."[12]

This is only one mild example of the prevailing attitudes of men toward women cited by Hamilton. Sad to say we still see remnants of such thinking in the church today which is contrary to the nature of God. Glen Scorgie, professor of theology at Bethel Seminary, says, "The dynamics of our experiences of being-in-relationship, including those with God and with one another as male and female, are meant to reflect something of the interior life of the triune God."[13] He states further, "How we relate to one another as women and men may be one of the most significant criteria by which our God-likeness can be judged to be restored."[14] The historical perspective of viewing women as inferior to men stems from "Judaism corrupted by Talmudic Laws. If a woman is considered mentally inferior to a man or suffering under the curse of Eve, that also is Pharisee-ism. Such prejudice and bias and attitudes of men towards women are indeed legalism in its worst form."[15] Relating to one another in the spirit of acceptance and respect for God's creation is a manifestation of humility. When we esteem ourselves as better than another, be that men above women or women above men, we will not be restored to fulfill God's mandate to us.

Discrimination of gender violates the nature of God. Galatians 3:28 makes it clear that just as there is no discrimination of race or class, neither is there discrimination of gender in Christ. Regarding our relationship to one another as the image of God, Matthew Henry comments, "Thus holy, thus happy, were our first parents, in having the image of God upon them. And this honour, put upon man at first, is a good reason why we should not speak ill one of another (James 3:9), nor do ill one to another (Gen. 9:6), and a good reason why we should not debase ourselves to the service of sin, and why we should devote ourselves to God's service."[16]

In the beginning, God desired male and female to live together in harmony fulfilling His mandates to them. Granted we fell (Chapter

4 deals with that), but Jesus was sent to redeem us. The Sinless One came to restore the image of God in us by bringing us into relationship with God. When we are re-created by faith in Jesus, we are in position to begin to live as God intended in the beginning. Will we continue to live as though the work of Christ was in vain? Fuchsia Pickett sums it up well.

> By the action of Calvary, we are being changed into Christ's image so male and female can walk together in their own realms of authority. God puts both genders back into Christ, not as male and female, but as mankind, walking with God. Husband and wife, male and female preacher, man and woman leader will walk in the cool of the day with Jesus, who is talking to us, fellowshipping with us, giving us authority and changing us into His image. In the "last Adam," God is restoring what we would have had if Adam had not fallen in the beginning.[17]

IMPLICATIONS FOR MEN AND WOMEN

As redeemed people, both genders must begin to recognize the image of God in them. Our personal perception of God affects our acceptance of others. When we see God as a "hard taskmaster" or "the almighty sheriff" who is out to get us, we perceive others as being against us. Authorities in our life, parents, guardians, teachers, pastors, may have contributed to our perception of God. Women who have been abused, emotionally or physically, by male authorities must be healed of their wounds and overcome the strongholds of their minds. Men who have been betrayed or controlled by female authorities must be healed of their wounds and overcome the strongholds of their minds. Allowing our past experiences to determine our future will limit God's purposes for our lives.

When we embrace the power of the cross to liberate us of negative relationships, our perception of God and others will allow us to see His image in each other. The cross of Jesus Christ is both vertical and horizontal. We must receive forgiveness from God for our attitudes and actions. Then we have forgiveness to forgive others of their attitudes and actions against us. Even when someone has been an innocent victim (which is not often) they usually harbor anger, bitterness and hatred toward the perpetrator. Such attitudes must be forgiven and cleansed from our lives before we can release forgiveness to others. Once we have been forgiven and released forgiveness, we are free to pursue God's purposes in our lives.

Several years ago when I was going through an onslaught of misunderstandings, I had a dream. In the dream, someone was throwing rocks at me. When I reached down to pick up a rock to throw back at them, I noticed a rope laying there. I picked up the rope, made a lasso and lassoed the person. I brought the rope down below their elbows so they could not pick up any more rocks. I remember holding the rope tight. Then I awakened. Sensing the presence of the Lord, I asked Him what he was trying to show me. It became clear that I was in as much bondage by holding on to the rope as the rock thrower. I would never be able to move forward holding on to the rope of revenge. Embracing the cross by receiving and releasing forgiveness is the most liberating force in the world!

Women, let go of your ropes against men. Men, let go of your ropes against women. God is calling us to be reconciled one to another. "Receive one another, even as Christ has received you" (Rom. 15:7). Know you are created in the image of God and accepted in Jesus Christ.

(Endnotes)

1   Biblesoft's New Exhaustive Strong's Numbers and Concordance with Expanded Greek-Hebrew Dictionary. (Biblesoft, Inc. and International Bible Translators, Inc.,1994, 2003).

2   Vine's Expository Dictionary of Biblical Words. Thomas Nelson Publishers, 1985.

3   Jeannette I. Wuest. Wuest's Word Studies from the Greek New Testament. Wm. B. Eerdmans Publishing Co., 1940-55, renewed 1968.

4   "Thayer's Greek Lexicon." Biblesoft, Inc. Electronic Database. 2000, 2003.

5   Ibid.

6   Theological Wordbook of the Old Testament. The Moody Bible Institute of Chicago, 1980.

7   Groothuis, Rebecca Merrill. Good News for Women. Baker Books, 1997, p. 101.

8   International Standard Bible Encyclopedia. Electronic Database. (Biblesoft, Inc., 1996, 2003)

9   Keil and Delitzsch Commentary on the Old Testament: New Updated Edition, Electronic Database. (Hendrickson Publishers, Inc., 1996).

10 Matthew Henry's Commentary on the Whole Bible: New Modern Edition. Electronic Database. (Hendrickson Publishers, Inc., 1991).

11 Spencer, Aida Bensancon. Beyond the Curse. Hendrickson Publishers, 1985, p. 21.

12 Cunningham, Loren, and David Hamilton. Why Not Women?. YWAM Publishing: Seattle, 2000, p. 106.

13 Scorgie, Glen. The Journey Back to Eden. Zondervan, 2005, p.63.

14 Ibid., p. 64.

15 Conner, Kevin J. The Ministry of Women. KJC Publications, 2003, p. 81.

16 Matthew Henry's Commentary on the Whole Bible: New Modern Edition. Electronic Database. (Hendrickson Publishers, Inc., 1991).

17 Pickett, Fuchsia. Male and Female: Created to Co-labor with God. Spiritledwoman.com/wim/picket.html

2

RULING TOGETHER

THEN GOD BLESSED THEM, AND GOD SAID TO THEM,
"BE FRUITFUL AND MULTIPLY; FILL THE EARTH AND SUBDUE
IT; HAVE DOMINION OVER THE FISH OF THE SEA, OVER THE
BIRDS OF THE AIR, AND OVER EVERY LIVING THING THAT
MOVES ON THE EARTH"
(GEN. 1:28).

In chapter one, we discussed Genesis 1:26-27. In verse 26 God declares, "Let us make man in Our image, according to our likeness; let *them* have dominion…" The next verse states, "So God created man in His own image…male and female created He them" (Gen. 1:27). In this chapter, we look at verse 28 which is God's specific orders to *them*. This commandment is actually the foundation of God's purpose for mankind to serve Him. Notice, He gave it to *them*, male and female. In this chapter, we will examine its meaning in two parts.

First is the command to "be fruitful and multiply". This command is given throughout Scripture to the people of God. It was repeated to Noah in Genesis 9:1 and 7 as his responsibility to replenish the earth after the flood. God is always desirous of generations to come and commands natural reproduction. Yet, these two words, fruitful and multiply, are linked in more ways than the natural, physical process of reproduction.

Three primary meanings of fruit are covered by the Hebrew language.

1. The fruit of a tree
2. The fruit of the womb
3. Fruit as consequences resulting from an action[1]

FRUIT OF A TREE

First, the fruit of a tree begins with a seed and contains seed in itself. The unique characteristic of fruit is that it contains seed. Even the banana has little tiny black specks that are seeds. Take the seed of an apple and plant an apple tree to produce more apples. When we receive the seed of the Word of God with faith, it will bring forth good fruit in our lives. Good seed produces good fruit. Good fruit comes from the tree of life which is the nature and character of God in our lives and ministries. Both men and women are mandated by God to be fruitful. God wants His nature exhibited in the lives of both men and women. The book of Galatians shows the clearest picture of His character as fruit, "But the fruit of the Spirit is love, joy, peace, longsuffering, kindness, goodness, faithfulness, gentleness, self-control (Gal. 5:22-23). These are not gender sensitive characteristics. They are the result of anyone abiding in the vine and living after the spirit rather than the flesh. As Christian men and women, our lives are to exhibit His nature or character. Character is not developed in isolation. Being in relationship with each other is "where the rubber meets the road". We are refined and sharpened in our relationships, especially male/female relationships.

In the course of forty years of ministry, the fruit of patience has been refined in my life. Interestingly, I recall patience being refined more often in my relationship to male leadership. I am called of God as a teacher and often women have not been perceived in that ministry. I have sat in 'silence and submission' for as long as a year and a few times longer until male leadership recognized the calling of God in my life. I am thankful for those times of refinement for I have more patience as a result. Granted, I will continue to be refined in that area of my life.

Relationships with our own gender have refining possibilities, but sometimes we tend to ignore or discount the significance of God's processing in us through relationships with the opposite sex. If we fail to value the opinions or gifts of the opposite sex, we will not consider those conflicts as God's refining process in us. We can be snared in pride by believing only "significant" relationships are worth resolving. Significant relationships usually include authorities over us and close friends. Yet, God will use anyone, anytime to reveal our weaknesses and help develop His strength in us.

FRUIT OF THE WOMB

The second characteristic is the fruit of the womb. The womb is the place of conception, where seed is fertilized to bring forth life. In natural life, birthing consists of conceiving and delivering. Delivery needs strength and encouragement. The birthing process goes much better when we work as a team in the physical and spiritual realm. It takes both man and woman in the natural, and it will take both, men and women, to produce a spiritual harvest of souls. C.P. DeYoung cites Steve Charleston's prediction:

In the next century, the Christian church is going to experience a second major reformation. It will be far more powerful than the one we knew in sixteenth century Europe. For one thing, it will be international, not just regional. It will cross over not only denominational lines, but also over lines of color, class, gender and age...While the West will participate in this reformation, it will not play a dominant role. The leaders of the coming reformation will be women. They will be from Africa, Asia, Latin America and Native America. They are being born right now.[2]

The Psalmist also predicted such a reformation. "The Lord gives the word [of power]; the women who bear and publish [the news] are a great host" (Ps. 68:11, AMP). Ed Silvoso brings this scripture to light in *Women, God's Secret Weapon*. God's great host of women is coming forth in this day. It is essential that women partner with men in this reformation.

When we enter into a gender balance of leadership, we will increase our fruitfulness in the earth. Barbara Yoder says it well. "Without women there will never be a harvest. They must come alongside men and begin to labor with them so that the fullness of the harvest can come. Until women get in their place, the harvest will be withheld."[3] Bringing forth new life in Christ is part of the mandate given to all believers. As Proverbs says, "The fruit of the righteous is a tree of life, and he who wins souls is wise" (Pro. 11:30). Witnessing to people by sharing the good news is not limited by gender. In fact the good news was often shared first by women in the Bible.

One example is the Samaritan woman in John 4. This encounter is an example of Jesus breaking traditions of a male dominated society. He joined a woman to share the good news for her life. What a breakthrough for the gospel as she went back to the men telling them of the One she met. Jesus was willing to use a woman to spread the gospel to an entire city (John 4:27-30). Spreading the good news of the gospel is an aspect of fruitfulness in which everyone can participate.

FRUIT AS CONSEQUENCES

The third definition of fruitfulness is the result of one's actions. Our actions or decisions will produce good or bad fruit. In the Garden of Eden there were two trees—one for life and one for death. Adam and Eve chose to eat of the wrong tree. God held them responsible for their individual actions, but those choices had corporate consequences as well. We all suffered the results of their disobedience. Thank God through Jesus we have been redeemed from the curse. Even so, the principle remains that our individual choices affect the corporate body. So our good choices or obedience to God produces good fruit and our bad choices or disobedience to God produces bad fruit. Others see and partake of the fruit of our lives and are blessed or hindered by our fruit.

The will and purpose of God for the present time is often new to us. God is always moving into the "new" as we know it. It may not be new to Him, but it is new to us. Bringing forth the new is an aspect of fruitfulness. When men and women join together, their ability to see and bring forth the "new thing" God wants to do is enhanced.

FRUITFUL PARTNERSHIP

We are living in such a time that God is bringing men and women together to accomplish His purposes. Prophet Chuck Pierce has been an example of this in our day. He says, "During the past decade I have had the opportunity to work with great women of faith. Through my position among the leaders in the global prayer movement, our Lord has brought me into relationship with several gifted women who know how to wield great authority on their knees."[4] God has used Chuck and the women God has partnered with him to bring forth a harvest of fruit in the earth. God knew from the beginning man and woman would have to work together to accomplish His purposes for them. The strengths of each one would be necessary to be fruitful and subdue and have dominion.

Jack Hayford raises a critical question in an article in *Spirit Led Woman* magazine.

> But if we are all equal, how is it that the church has so often been guilty of sanctifying a chauvinistic system in which women are put--and not always gently--in second place? I believe it is time for us to revisit the issue of what a woman's place is in God's order of things.[5]

When it comes to principles of leading, ruling, subduing or having dominion, we have often drawn gender lines. God obviously did not draw any lines in the beginning. I believe God sent Jesus Christ so we could live according to His original intent. We have allowed sin and its consequences to determine how we live even though we have entered into the new covenant through faith in Jesus Christ. We are one in Christ. We all came the same path by grace through faith in Jesus.

Gretchen Gaebelein Hull says it this way, "When Adam said of Eve, 'This is…flesh of my flesh,' the words connoted oneness, not separation, and certainly not inequality, lesser gifts or limited role. Genesis 1:26-30 tells us that as originally created; both men and women were to rule the earth mutually and cooperatively."[6] She goes on to point out, "The Bible does not present one set of redemptive truths for males and another set for females." As redeemed men and women, we must cease discriminating against one another and begin to join together in fulfilling God's command to us. We must cease the dual and become a duet, a gender blended partnership.

BE FRUITFUL AND RULE...TOGETHER

The Lausaunne Committee for World Evangelization hosted a forum in 2004 on *Empowering Men and Women to Use Their Gifts Together in Advancing the Gospel*. In Occasional Paper No. 53 Chad and Leslie Neal Seagraves state, "Because God's design was for men and women to serve side-by-side, Satan fights to maintain the hierarchy that places men over women. However, when the Church recaptures God's original intent, the unity will result in a great harvest of souls through the earth." Cindy Jacobs writes of this hindrance to harvest "one of the saddest results of the patriarchal spirit is that it prohibits men and women from working together in team ministry. I believe God desires to heal the gender gap so we can come together to minister, reach the lost and bring forth fruitfulness in the generations."[7]

Examination of a biblical view of leadership is essential for our fulfilling the commandment to be fruitful and rule together. A hierarchal/patriarchal view of leadership has it roots in ancient pagan religions. Susan Hyatt gives a thorough historical perspective on the development of orthodox theology. She states:

> The development of the Church's 'orthodox theology' – or acceptable way of thinking about things-disregarded Jesus' teaching about women. Perhaps this is because this sanctioned way of thinking evolved in the minds of men who were converts from paganism…their minds had been molded by the pagan, Greco-Roman philosophies in which they had previously excelled.[8]

We must recognize the strongholds that exist in our theology that are totally contrary to the mind of Christ. Hyatt goes on to say, "This problem intensified when Thomas Aquinas (1125-1274) systematized Roman theology using Aristotelian philosophy. Thus the male superiority/female inferiority, male rulership/female subjugation, male dominance/female silence formula was established in the root system of orthodox theology" (p. 56). Lee Grady cites several quotes of ancient church leaders in his book, *Ten Lies the Church Tells Women*. "God maintained the order of each sex by dividing the business of life into two parts and assigned the more necessary and beneficial aspects to the man and the less important, inferior matters to the woman.—Early Church Father John Chrysostom (A.D. 347-407)."[9]

Such patriarchal thinking was not God's intent in the garden. Grady gives another quote from Thomas Acquinas, thirteenth-century theologian. "…Woman is in subjection according to the law of nature, but a slave is not, Children ought to love their father more than their mother" (p. 68). Most of us would think how ridiculous, yet the roots of such thinking still have sprouts in the church.

Gilbert Bilezikian makes a good point regarding the mandate

to rule the earth. "Since both man and woman bear the image of God, they are both assigned the task of ruling the earth, without any reference to differentiation on the basis of sex." He further clarifies this, "The whole created universe—from the stars in space to the fish in the sea—is carefully organized in a hierarchy of order that is meticulously defined in Genesis 1. And yet, there is not the slightest indication that such a hierarchy existed between Adam and Eve."[10] In fact, as the redeemed people of God, Scripture exhorts us regarding our relationship one with another. Jesus said, "You know that the rulers of the Gentiles lord it over them, and those who are great exercise authority over them. Yet it shall not be so among you; but whoever desires to become great among you, let him be your servant" (Matt. 20:25-27). Then we are exhorted by Paul in Colossians 3:12-14. "Therefore, as the elect of God, holy and beloved, put on tender mercies, kindness, humility, meekness, longsuffering; bearing with one another, and forgiving one another, if anyone has a complaint against another; even as Christ forgave you, so you also must do. But above all these things put on love, which is the bond of perfection".

Obeying such exhortations will eliminate the power struggles in relationships and enable us to overcome the temptations of the Evil One. Though Adam and Eve failed to obey the mandate to subdue the earth and have dominion over the creatures, Jesus has given us authority to fulfill the command. Yet, we have neglected this command also. Romans chapter eight gives us the consequences of our negligence.

> For the earnest expectation of the creation eagerly waits for the revealing of the sons of God. For the creation was subjected to futility, not willingly, but because of Him who subjected it in hope; because the creation itself also will be delivered

from the bondage of corruption into the glorious liberty of the children of God. For we know that the whole creation groans and labors with birth pangs together until now. (Rom. 8:19-23)

What a sobering thought that creation itself is waiting for us, the sons (children) of God to be revealed for who we were created to be. Keil and Delitzsch comment on this passage. "The fact which now prevails universally in nature and the order of the world, the violent and often painful destruction of life, is not a primary law of nature, nor a divine institution founded in the creation itself, but entered the world along with death at the fall of man, and became a necessity of nature through the curse of sin."[11]

Since sin is what brought the curse on creation, only sinlessness can redeem it from the curse. Jesus, the Sinless One, has redeemed us, his created people, from the curse that we might liberate creation from its curse. When we are conspicuously the children of God and take dominion over the curse, we will see the beginning of the fulfillment of Romans 8. I acknowledge that the final fulfillment of earth's restoration will be manifested in Christ's return, but we do have a part to play in that restoration now.

FRUITFUL AND FREE

God created us free. Free to worship Him. Male and female were created in duality to have constant, open communion with God. They were free to honor and obey God. Their obedience to God was to be like Him in that they were to rule the creatures. Deitrich Bonhoeffer, a German theologian of the early 1900's, says it this way.

Man in duality—man and woman—is brought into the world of the fixed and the living in his likeness to God. And just as his freedom over against man consisted in the fact that he was to be free *for* him, his freedom over against the rest of the created world is to be free *from* it. That means that he is its master, he has command over it, he rules it. And here is the other side of man's created likeness to God. Man is to rule—of course as over God's creation, as one who receives the commission and power of his dominion from God."[12]

We can only rule over what we have mastered. When we yield ourselves to the control of anything in this world, we are ruled by it. To fulfill God's mandate to us, we must live free from the rest of creation in order to exercise dominion over it. Bonhoeffer sums this up, "Man's being free for God and the other person and his being-free-from the creature, in his dominion over it, is the image of God in the first man" (p. 40).

Being free in God through Christ enables us to serve one another. When men and women function together greater, authority to subdue is realized. The enemy has resisted this cooperation forever. He must know that once male and female subdue the cursed earth and take dominion over the enemy, his rule is over. "The word for subdue is k'baš, and it assumes that the party being subdued is hostile to the subduer, necessitating some sort of coercion if the subduing is to take place."[13] We, the children of God, have a hostile enemy who must be subdued at every opportunity. It is essential for us to understand that we are not subduing one another, but we are to subdue the enemy, Satan. God gave this command to Adam and Eve knowing that the serpent would come to them, and they would need to rule over him. But God also knew they would fail to obey the command to rule. He sent Jesus to redeem us so we can fulfill His mandate. Shall we continue the pattern of domination of one another or rise up as men and women to rule over the enemy and gather a harvest?

IMPLICATIONS FOR MEN AND WOMEN

First, let us teach biblical equality of men and women as God's original intent. Once we have been forgiven and forgiven of the past, renewing our minds with truth will enable us to move forward. Change comes as our thinking changes. We can make ourselves act differently but if there is not a change of mind, behavioral change will be temporary. Teaching revelation of God's original purposes for mankind releases a fresh anointing to embrace what God is calling us to in this day – to rule and take dominion in the earth.

Second, men and women must begin to lay down what we thought were our rights at the feet of Jesus and take up a servant model of ruling. We rule over a common enemy not each other. Domination and control of one another violate God's principle of leading. God, Himself, allowed us free will. He gave us the privilege of decision making for ourselves. God does not lead us by coercion or domination. We resent dictatorial leadership because it is not God's way. Female dictators are as wrong as male dictators. We must be willing to serve one another by yielding to the gift and anointing of God in each other. There are times when the appointed leader submits to the wisdom or anointing of a follower. No one person holds all the authority in themselves. We are not *independent,* but *interdependent* as the Body of Christ.

God created male and female to complement each other. Men

are not complete by themselves, but neither are women complete without men. In the church, we *compete* with each other rather than *complete* each other. This is not only true of opposite sexes, but even within our own genders, we compete with each other. Competition competes for power and position. Jesus knew who He was and His mission on earth; therefore, He never competed with anyone. When we know who we are and our purpose on earth, we have no need to compare or compete with one another. In fact, our security in Christ can eliminate the three C's that have hindered us - Control, Competition and Comparison. Have a renewal of your own mind as to who God is in you! Accept your gifts and callings. Know your boundaries and be content to serve the Body of Christ within your sphere of authority.

(Endnotes)
1   *Theological Wordbook of the Old Testament.* The Moody Bible Institute of Chicago, 1980.
2   DeYoung, Curtiss Paul. *Coming Together.* Judson Press: Valley Forge, PA, 1995 p. 188.
3   Yoder, Barbara J. *God's Bold Call to Women.* Regal Publishers, 2005, p. 67.
4   Pierce, Chuck and Rebecca Wagner Sytsema. *Future War of the Church.* Renew Publishers, 2001, p. 235.
5   Hayford, Jack. *A Woman's Place in Christ.*
6   Hull, Gretchen Gaebelein. *Equal to Serve.* Baker Book House, 1998, p.80.
7   Jacobs, Cindy. *Responding to the Patriarchal Spirit.* Spiritledwoman.com/wim/slw100010.html
8   Hyatt, Susan. *In the Spirit We Are Equal.* Hyatt Press, 1998, p. 49.
9   Grady, Lee. *Ten Lies the Church Tells Women.* Creation House, 2000, p. 30.
10 Bilezikian, Gilbert. *Beyond Sex Roles,* Baker Book House, 1985. p. 24.
11 Keil and Delitzsch Commentary on the Old Testament: New Updated Edition, Electronic Database. (Hendrickson Publishers, Inc., 1996).
12 Bonhoeffer, Dietrich. *Creation and the Fall.* Macmillan Company, 1959, p.37.
13 Ibid. endnote 1

3

WORKING TOGETHER

"IT IS NOT GOOD THAT MAN SHOULD BE ALONE"
(GEN. 2:18).

God's original mandate to humankind could never be realized without Adam receiving his helper. When Adam was "alone" in the garden, God commanded him not to eat of the tree of the knowledge of good and evil, or he would surely die (Gen. 2:17). Immediately after that command, God said He would make him a helper suitable for him.

What is the meaning of this helper God gave man? The original definition of woman's role is a bit different from the perspective I have known. Growing up in church, I came to understand and witness woman as a helper who performed menial tasks for a man. She was at his beck and call. Man called, and woman jumped. As we look at the original meaning of the word, we find a different perspective.

The Hebrew word for helper is ¢zer. It is defined in this way: "While this word designates assistance, it is more frequently used in a concrete sense to designate the assistant (Cf. Gen. 2:18, 20 – where Eve is created to be Adam's help[er]). As to the source of the help, this word is generally used to designate divine aid, particularly in Psalms (Cf. Ps. 121:1, 2) where it includes both material and spiritual assistance."[1]

In other words, *helper* is the same word used for God as our *helper*. That gives us some insight into the role of *helper* for man. We could look at many scripture references to God as our helper. Let Psalm 121:2 suffice: "My help comes from the Lord, who made heaven and earth."

The word *meet* in the King James Version sheds further light on the term *helper*. Adam Clarke comments on it this way: "It is not good that the man should be alone, ªbadow; only himself, I will make him a help meet for him; `eezer kªnegªdow, "a help, a counterpart of himself," one formed from him, and a perfect resemblance of his person. If the word be rendered scrupulously literally, it signifies one like or as himself standing opposite to or before him. This implies that the woman was to be a perfect resemblance of the man possessing neither inferiority nor superiority but being in all things like and equal to himself."[2]

These original definitions shed light on the concept of woman being the *helper* of man. She was to be equal and able to help him in his tasks. There is no indication from these meanings that she would be inferior to him or necessarily in subjection to him. Consider that God is one who helps us. We do not conclude that He is in subjection to us. The same word is used for the *helper* God gave Adam.

Some would use the "order of creation" to establish male dominance over woman, in that man was created first. Susan Hyatt points out, "If, however, 'order of creation' establishes male dominance, then it follows that the animals should have authority over man since they were created prior to man. In fact, nothing in the passage suggests that God provided for or intended male dominance of authority over woman. Instead, it is obvious in both Genesis 1 and 2 that God has set up an interdependence of equal partnership".[3] Chuck Pierce confirms this. "Truly whatever seeks to demean, enslave or dominate women is contrary to God's original plan and purpose for humankind. Man and woman were created equal in all aspects."[4]

HOLY SPIRIT AS HELPER

We can also look at the word *helper* in the New Testament and find it is used in reference to the Holy Spirit (John 14). The New Testament word is *paraclete*, one who comes alongside. A helper is one who comes alongside another to help in a specific task. Is it not possible that the helper God gave Adam was intended to be an assistant equal to him as she comes alongside him? Our relationship with the Holy Spirit is certainly not independent of Him, but interdependently we work together to accomplish God's purposes in our lives. We need the help of the Holy Spirit, and God ordained the Holy Spirit to work through us. By the aid of the Holy Spirit, we can accomplish the tasks in the earth God has given us to do. Likewise, God gave man a woman to be an equal help in all the tasks God gave them.

Scorgie summarizes the meaning of *ezer* as "a partner corresponding to him". He concludes further, "The most natural reading of the text, then, is to conclude that the woman, as a helper corresponding to the man, as his equal, is to partner with him in the fulfillment of the creation mandate in its broadest dimensions."[5] Furthermore if she is a helper in the tasks, she is actually doing the same thing as the one she is helping. When men and women work together at the same task they are accomplishing the same goal. Man could not fulfill the commandment to be fruitful and multiply without woman. This is equally true in fulfilling the goal of multiplying the church. God is calling for the multiplication of believers and churches, and he will use the genders working together to accomplish it.

SINGLE HELPER

A word here to single men and women – You are included as the creation of God. Paul validates the place for single men and women to serve the Lord. "There is a difference between a wife and a virgin. The unmarried woman cares about the things of the Lord that she may be holy both in body and in spirit. But she who is married cares about the things of the world — how she may please her husband" (1 Cor. 7:34). Bilezikian says of this passage, "Single women were able to act as independent agents, not deriving their identities from a spouse or a male relative. They could choose to devote themselves to Christian service on the same basis as their male counterparts."[6] How often in the church we have overlooked single women for equal opportunity to exercise their gifts. Have we subconsciously considered them unfit because they were not married? Do we see them only as in need of help from the church? God forbid that we would neglect the great potential there is in the increasing number of single women in the church.

WORLD VIEW OF HELPER

How interesting that the corporate and political world have begun to embrace gender balanced leadership before the church does. In the course of researching this topic, I have been amazed at the plethora of literature related to men and women in leadership. My husband brought home a magazine he found at a meeting he was attending in downtown Atlanta. The magazine titled, *Atlanta Woman—Bold, Balanced, Beautiful*. The January 2005 issue was entitled, "25 Power Women to Watch". The issue consists of interviews and articles of these 25 women who are executives in the corporate world of Atlanta, obviously working with a male staff.

The same week in Atlanta the "first lady of the civil rights movement" died. The Atlanta Journal, February 1, 2006 said of Coretta Scott King, "She didn't walk behind her husband, she walked beside him…She was the woman who shaped his ideas and activism and she single-handedly maintained his legacy."[7]

Former President Jimmy Carter included a chapter on men and women in his book, *Our Endangered Values*. He observes, "It is ironic that women are now welcomed into all major professions and other positions of leadership but are deprived of the right to serve Jesus Christ in positions of leadership as they did during his early ministry and in the early Christian churches."[8] Women in our day will rise up to be who they are called to be. If not in the church, they will go outside the church. If they can work together with men as equals in the workplace, how much more should it be a reality in the church?

BIBLICAL HELPERS

There are several male – female teams that worked together in the Bible – Miriam with Moses and Aaron, Deborah and Barak, Esther and Mordecai, Abigail and David to name a few from the Old Testament. In the New Testament, we have the women who traveled and ministered with Jesus and Paul. Women headed house churches -

Chloe, Nemphia, Lydia, Apphia. Priscilla and Aquila, Andronicus and Junia were teachers and apostles; Philip's daughters were prophets.

Throughout history, there are many examples of men and women working together for the sake of the gospel. Loren Cunningham cites the spiritual awakening in the late 1700 and early 1800's. "The Wesley brothers had a remarkable, godly mother named Susanna. Besides spending time every day in earnest prayer, Susanna found time to teach each one of her nine surviving children. Mrs. Wesley preached to more than two hundred people every week in prayer meetings which she led in her husband's parish."[9] We see women throughout history leading in movements affecting society. From Joan of Arc to Margaret Fell, co-founder of the Quakers, to Catherine Booth, co-founder of the Christian Mission and the Salvation Army, to Aimee Simple McPherson, founder of the Four Square denomination. The history of Christian missions also has a long legacy of women missionaries. In China alone, twice as many women as men marched into China as missionaries. Because women were hindered from teaching men in the Bible schools, they taught women in their homes and by the rivers as they washed their clothes. Today the majority of the house churches in China are led by women.[10]

It is interesting that throughout history we see the rise of leadership among women in the Church during times of Holy Spirit outpourings. What a fulfillment of Joel's prophecy. "And it shall come to pass afterward that I will pour out My Spirit on all flesh; Your sons and your daughters shall prophesy, Your old men shall dream dreams, Your young men shall see visions. And also on My menservants and on My maidservants I will pour out My Spirit in those days (Joel 2:28-29). May we experience fresh outpourings of the Spirit in this day, anointing us to be co-laborers together for the sake of the Gospel.

HELPERS RECONCILED

We are in need of receiving the ministry of reconciliation between genders. God ordained from the beginning that we would work together to build the Kingdom of God. We are not to walk isolated or hostile to one another. Our preconceived ideas of the opposite sex must be replaced with a renewed mind, the mind of Christ. We are one in Christ.

Because there are some "difficult passages" related to women serving in ministry, we want to look at one scripture that is very clear. Dr. J. Robert Clinton makes a valid point in trying to understand or interpret Scripture. His first principal of interpreting Scripture is "interpret unclear passages in light of clear ones—not the other way around. Major doctrines should flow from what is clear."[11]

One clear scripture regarding our faith in Christ and the "oneness" He came to restore is Galatians 3:28. "There is neither Jew nor Greek; there is neither slave nor free, there is neither male nor female; for you are all one in Christ Jesus". The context of this verse is comparing the Old Covenant with the New Covenant of Christ. Under the Law there were religious categories of ethnicity – Jew and Gentile, social class – slave and free, and gender – male and female. All three of these groups suffered laws of inequality. Rights and privileges were determined by one's ethnicity, social class or gender. The New Covenant in Christ is vastly different. It is obvious that Christ came to fulfill the law and that as children of God we are no longer under the curse of the law. Faith has come, and when we enter into faith in Christ we become one in Him. In Christ, there is no favoritism for one group over another.

James states clearly, "If you really fulfill the royal law according to the Scripture, 'you shall love your neighbor as yourself,' you do well; but if you show partiality, you commit sin, and are convicted by the law as transgressors" (James 2:8-9). We now live under the royal law of love as equal partners in the grace of God. Christ closed all the gaps of sin, first and foremost. When sin is dealt with, every other gap, be it gender, ethnic or social, can be overcome. Christ gave abundant life to all. The Law and its curses are done away with by faith in Christ. The law we now live by is the law of love and acceptance. Mindsets that once separated us have been demolished.

Paul speaks of the abolishment of the enmity between Jew and Gentile, "For He Himself is our peace, who has made both one, and has broken down the middle wall of separation, having abolished in His flesh the enmity, that is, the law of commandments contained in ordinances, so as to create in Himself one new man from the two, thus making peace, and that He might reconcile them both to God in one body through the cross, thereby putting to death the enmity" (Eph. 2:14). The power of the cross of Jesus Christ has broken all "walls of hostility" (AMP). The wall of hostility between genders began with the sin of the first male and female. Jesus Christ is the great reconciler of genders. Every "male hating" attitude or "woman hating" attitude must be abolished. Men are to be men and women are to be women fulfilling their God-given destinies. Christ made it possible for us to come together in His body and fulfill His purposes in the earth. Throughout history, we have seen the manifestation of walls of hostility and prejudice breaking between God's people. Now is the time for the genders to partner together as never before.

Former President Jimmy Carter sums up this issue. "Devout

Christians can find adequate Scripture to justify either side in this debate. The question is whether we, evangelical believers in Christ, want to abandon his example and exclude a vast array of potential female partners, who are equally devoted and responding to God's call to serve with us in advancing God's kingdom on earth."[12]

IMPLICATIONS FOR MEN AND WOMEN

We must identify personal resistance to the truth of equality. Consider the "if's" you have been thinking – if women would…if men would…God accepts each of us individually, and we must do the same. We are more likely to generalize the opposite sex when we have been wounded and not been healed. Working with male leaders in the church has allowed me the opportunity to hear many horrendous stories of women's attempts to get their own way. By the same token, I have witnessed male leaders unwilling to trust women or receive any counsel from them. Issues of respect and honor often indicate unresolved issues in our lives. Our relationships within our own parents or marriages may need to be resolved and healed. Anyone, male or female, who engages in manipulation, control or independence has difficulty being an effective team player. Working together requires trust and respect of one another. If you need to prove yourself trustworthy, do so by respecting the other person.

How willing are we to take specific steps toward reconciliation? Ask the Holy Spirit to reveal bias attitudes you hold toward the opposite sex. Receive forgiveness from God and others.

Take a step of faith and ask a member of the opposite sex to help you in a task. Balance ministry teams by having both male and

CHAPTER THREE

female on each team. Appoint a gifted woman to lead a male team.
Appoint a man to serve on the women's ministry council.

Talk of the need for men and women working together can
go on forever. Until we begin to practice what we are saying, nothing
will change. God's mandate for humankind to take dominion must be
obeyed.

(Endnotes)
1   Theological Wordbook of the Old Testament. The Moody Bible Institute of Chicago, 1980.
2   Adam Clarke's Commentary. Electronic Database. (Biblesoft, Inc., 1996, 2003).
3   Hyatt, Susan. In the Spirit We Are Equal. Hyatt Press, 1998, p. 234.
4   Pierce, Chuck and Rebecca Wagner Sytsema. Future War of the Church. Renew Publishers, 2001, p. 243.
5   Scorgie, Glen. The Journey Back to Eden. Zondervan, 2005, p.73.
6   Bilezikian, Gilbert. Beyond Sex Roles, Baker Book House, 1985. p. 134.
7   Suggs, Ernie. Portrait of Dignity. p. A13.
8   Carter, Jimmy. Our Endangered Values. Simon and Schuster, 2005, p. 90.
9   Cunningham, Loren. Why Not Women? p. 25.
10   Ibid., p. 26.
11   Clinton, J. Robert. Gender and Leadership Article, Barnabas Publishers Reprint, 1995, p 24.
12   Carter. Ibid. p. 93.

4

FAILED TOGETHER

"SO WHEN THE WOMAN SAW THAT THE TREE WAS GOOD FOR
FOOD, THAT IT WAS PLEASANT TO THE EYES,
AND A TREE DESIRABLE TO MAKE ONE WISE,
SHE TOOK OF ITS FRUIT AND ATE. SHE ALSO GAVE
TO HER HUSBAND WITH HER, AND HE ATE"
(GEN. 3:6).

Adam and Eve were in verbal communication with God and each other. Their lives were lived in the presence of God, a paradise of glory. None of the creatures could speak their language until the serpent spoke to Eve. I will not look at the entirety of the temptation and disobedience, but only note a few aspects as it applies to our subject. This original tactic or temptation of the enemy is foundational to all his temptations with humankind. As leaders, we are not exempt from these same temptations. In verse 5, the sequence begins by bringing doubt to what God said. "Doubt, unbelief, and pride were the roots of the sin of our first parents, as they have been of all the sins of their posterity."[1] When God commands or enlightens us with truth for our lives, the enemy will tempt us as he did Eve by questioning what God said to us. When we yield to that thought, we begin to believe we can be as God, and pride leads us into greater deception.

In verse 6, we see a parallel to 1 John 2:16. "For all that is in the world, the lust of the flesh, and the lust of the eyes, and the pride of life, is not of the Father, but is of the world." Woman was being tempted with her natural appetite, her eyes and desire for wisdom or power. As leaders, all aspects of this temptation are vulnerable areas for us, in particular the pride of life. We must remember; the serpent was operating in the spirit of the fallen one who was cast down from heaven because of self exaltation (Is. 14). He continues to manifest in the same spirit, especially to leaders. If we see leadership as a place of power, then pride will bring us down. Leadership is a place of service, and we must walk humbly in it. Pride keeps prejudice and inequality in place and God hates it (Pro. 6:17, Ps. 101:5). The response of Adam and Eve to God's confrontation of their sin demonstrates that pride entered their relationship. We can not and will not live in harmony, anymore than Adam and Eve did, after yielding to temptation.

It is essential for us to see in this verse that Adam and Eve were together in their sin. For years, we have been led to believe it was all Eve's fault. Women are easily deceived, and therefore, can not be trusted. "Once again the Bible story stands in sharp contrast to the Greek myths. Evil didn't enter the world through one woman, Pandora. It entered through a human couple. Both were present. Both participated. Both were guilty before God, and both would suffer the consequences."[2]

Several observations from Genesis 3 should be noted. One is that they both sinned. God holds both of them accountable. Second, their responses to God are different. Third, the consequences of their sin are unique. In addition, I had a major question regarding why the serpent went for Eve, when God instructed Adam before Eve came on the scene. The question of why the serpent addressed Eve directly, even though Adam was there "with her" may be answered in verse 20. "And Adam called his wife's name Eve because she was the mother of all living" (Gen. 3:20).

WOMAN AS LIFE-GIVER

We have heard it said, "They are just living up to their name." My mother had no idea what my name meant when she named me Frances, but I have lived up to being a "free one." A name signifies the character and destiny of the one named. Adam named Eve and her name means life or life giving, mother of all living. Adam called his wife's name "Life" because she was to be the mother of all human beings, and because she was to be the mother of Him who was to give life to a world dead in trespasses and sin.[3] The first woman, Eve, was given her destiny in God – to bring forth life. Created in the image of God, who is the source of all life, Eve, was given the ability to carry life. Life comes forth from seed. Whether human, animal or plant life, it all begins with a seed. "It was through the power of divine grace that Adam believed the promise with regard to the woman's seed and manifested his faith in the name which he gave to his wife. "…This name was given by Adam to his wife, 'because,' as the writer explains with the historical fulfillment before his mind, "she became the mother of all living," i.e., because the continuance and life of his race were guaranteed to the man through the woman."[4]

Contrary to ancient beliefs, women do bear the life-giving seed. Loren Cunningham states, "The ancients believed that male semen contained tiny human beings that had been formed in a man's head. This belief led to the Greek "headship" concept. The woman was only the "soil" for the miniature human to grow in until birth."[5] If woman did not contain seed then why did God in His great plan of redemption choose to use only a woman to bring forth life? Jesus born of the seed of a woman was to be life for all humanity. The serpent went for the life giving one and yet God turned the tables on the enemy. "As woman lives out the affects of sin she "becomes an instrument for redemption rather than damnation."[6] Thank God who has redeemed all mankind from the curse of sin.

In Scripture, seed is not just natural, physical seed, but the Word of God and faith are referred to as seed. The Word or seed of God is life giving. Women pregnant with the Word and promises of God will carry faith in their spirits until they see it brought forth. Now as children of God, men also bring forth life from the seed God gives them. My husband is a visionary. He has received several visions from God that required his birthing schools and training programs for leaders. The vision doesn't come to pass only by receiving it. It has to be birthed and that requires struggle and travail which the responsibility of travail has fallen to me. So he speaks vision, and I travail until it comes forth. Both male and female are needed to bring forth what God desires. Women cannot give life alone. Men can not birth alone.

So why did the serpent tempt the woman? For years, I believed it was because she was easily deceived, but now I see that it was because she was the life giver. If the enemy could capture her, he would have the generations to come. It was the woman who was going to bring forth life from the seed within her–even eternal life through Jesus Christ. John and Stasi Eldredge describe Eve as "his (Satan's) greatest human threat, for she brings life."[7] The enemy has not changed. He still wants the seed of woman. He does not want women to fulfill their destiny to bring forth life. In the natural realm, the enemy is after the generations by trying to stop the life flow. So we have seen an increase in infertility and legalization of abortion.

Oppression and sexual violence against women are rampant around the world.

In the natural, we know life is to be conceived through intimate relations of husband and wife. In the spirit dimension, life is brought forth through intimacy with God. We accept His love for us and are born again by the spirit. The scripture also teaches that we can receive the word and bring forth life. "The words I speak they are spirit and life" (John 6:63). The word is seed in us. Creativity and life giving ideas thrive in open, honest relationships with God and each other. When we allow sin to rob us of our intimate relationship with God and each other, we will not have life giving seed. So what Satan was really after was their relationship with God and each other. He is still after that in us.

SIN IN THE GARDEN

Beyond that question, we need to note my original three points of this passage. First, both Adam and Eve sinned according to Genesis 3. Adam was guilty of eating the forbidden fruit. He ate knowing what God had commanded him. He knew first hand what the result of the disobedience would be. Adam received instruction directly from God before Eve was formed. When we know what is right and disobey it, we have sinned (James 4:17). Both Adam and Eve knew what was right and disobeyed God. They are both guilty before their Maker.

Second, we consider the confrontation of God to each of them regarding their sin. Have you ever noticed that God first confronts Adam rather than Eve who ate first? Some would say that is because he was responsible for both of them. Glen Scorgie says, "When

God finally connects with the furtive Adam, he does not hold him accountable for what they did, but only for what he did. God then turns to the woman and asks her to give an account of herself. It seems very clear that Adam and Eve are treated as separate moral agents, each with a direct and independent relationship to God."8 Is this not a picture of the priesthood of believers given us in Christ? Because of Christ we all have access to God and are directly responsible for our own sins. No one else will answer to God for you. You are responsible for your own decisions.

Adam responded to God in what has been perpetuated even until now – blame someone else. He did not just blame the woman, but he blamed God for giving her to him. "The woman whom You gave to be with me, she gave me of the tree, and I ate" (Genesis 3:12). It is amazing how easy it is for us to fall into the blame game. In our house when we hear "Well, you…." We can say, "Hello, Adam!" Most women would readily say that it is a common male thing, but we are guilty too. It is a human thing of our flesh, pointing the finger at someone else, instead of honest confession and receiving the blood covering for our sins.

When God confronted Eve we hear a similar but different response. "And the LORD God said to the woman, "What is this you have done?" The woman said, "The serpent deceived me, and I ate" (Gen. 3:13). Eve blames the serpent and boldly confesses her own choice to eat of the forbidden. Yet, in blaming the serpent she identifies him as the deceiver. We have no indication that he has been identified as such before this. He was described as subtle and cunning, but just in the text, not in conversation with Adam and Eve (Gen. 3:1). I find it significant that Eve names him for who he is –Deceiver. Though she was deceived her identifying him may be the more important issue.

ENEMY REVEALED

Ed Silvoso confirms another meaning of Eve's name in his book, *Women God's Secret Weapon*. "When the scripture describes Eve as "suitable helper" in ancient Hebrew it means "the revealer of the enemy".[9] What a helper! One who comes alongside to help by discerning the enemy! Is it no wonder women get upset when they see the enemy bringing havoc to the their homes, cities and nations? Yet it is this "help" of discerning the enemy's encroachment that is often a source of conflict between men and women. Many times women have discerned the enemy, but found such help is not wanted. Leaders do not always appreciate someone telling them the enemy is working. We do have biblical examples of women "helping" men by discerning the enemy. The story of Esther is an example of a woman being in position to warn a leader of evil. She was able to specifically reveal the enemy and have him hung. Pilate's wife is another example of a discerning woman who warned her husband. Jael, in the story of Deborah, not only knew the enemy but dealt directly with him.

When Eve called the serpent for who he was, the Lord turned to the serpent and cursed him. What you reveal God can deal with. Woman became the enemy's enemy. It is here in the beginning that God determined the battle of the ages. God made it clear to the serpent that from now on woman will hate you. "I will put enmity between you and the woman" (Gen. 3:15).

God knew He was going to redeem his creation from the fall and use woman to do it. The Deceiver may have intended to destroy woman and her seed, but God turned the tables on the enemy. From that day the serpent would hate the woman, and the woman would hate the serpent. War was declared by God Himself, and it continues to the end of the book of Revelation. The victory was won by Jesus! We see how He brought woman into her place because the Life He came to give could not be accomplished without woman.

BROKEN RELATIONSHIP

After cursing the serpent and declaring war, God turned to Eve and told her the consequences of her sin. She will suffer pain in the bearing of life, her desire shall be for her husband, and he shall rule over her (Gen. 3:16). David Hamilton says, "This was no command. God was simply describing the consequences of sin. God never intended Genesis 3:16 to become our guide for life and relationships. There was no command in this passage for Eve to submit to Adam—Eve was merely told the great impact sin would have on her world."[10] Stay with me while we consider three things in this verse. One – this was said by God after sin was committed. Sin affected Adam and Eve's relationship and still affects our relationships with each other. God created them to live in unity and obedience to His plan.

Kevin Conner summarizes the effects of the fall in his book, *The Ministry of Women.* "Sin brought about 'Gender Wars' and the 'Battle of the Sexes' entered the human race with the original man and woman. Mindsets like male chauvinism and secular feminism are a result of the Fall. The Fall brought about division and dominance which resulted in a broken, fractured relationship."[11] Through Jesus, God has provided for us to live according to His original plan.

Second, as a result of sin, Eve would desire or long for her husband more than for God. God is to be first and foremost the Lord of our lives. We choose to submit our lives to His will. God is our supreme leader. Submission to delegated authorities should never violate God's Word. We submit first to God. We are all called to live in submission to Him and the authorities of our lives. Submission is not the issue in this verse, but where is your desire or longing? Before Eve sinned, her desire was for God and communion with Him. The consequence of sin is that our desire for God as supreme will be diminished.

Third, as a result of sin Adam would have the opportunity to rule over her. Sin opens the door for oppression and domination. God never coerces anyone. He neither suppresses nor oppresses people. Sin oppresses and suppresses. Conner further states, "God did not command Adam to rule Eve. He simply told her what would happen. It was a prophecy of what would be. It was not His perfect will. Man's rule over his wife was not God's original intention. It came as a result of the Fall."[12]

The command to subdue and have dominion was to be over the creatures and the earth, not each other. This is the part we have often abused by attempting to dominate each other. Though we can see historical evidence of a "patriarchal" society and philosophies that have affected our interpretations of the Bible, matriarchy has also existed. Male dominance may have been evident in public life historically, but female dominance was present in private life. Dominance of each other is not God's plan.

God's judgment on Adam's sin was that he would work the cursed ground until he dies (Gen. 3:17-19). Lee Grady states, "These solemn words refer to the curse of poverty—the tragic economic depravity that rules every pagan culture. But we don't use this verse to teach that abject poverty is God's perfect will for men any more than we believe that because of Genesis 3:17-19 that all males should have agricultural occupations." Likewise we should not teach or practice the domination and oppression of women as the will of God. He goes on to say, "God created woman primarily to have fellowship with Him, yet we often try to define her worth and value only in terms of what she can do for her husband."[13]

A major result of the fall was a disruption of the unity man and woman shared with each other and with God. This is not God's way. It is the result of sin. Abuse of power and oppression of women is rampant in our world as a result of sin. Scorgie makes an interesting observation, "We should make no mistake about it: right here is where gender hierarchy originated...Prior to this specific moment of judgment there was no such thing."[14] As believers redeemed from the curse of sin, we should be living as God intended in the beginning before the fall. God commanded us in the beginning to live as male and female in communion with Him and one another, so we can be fruitful and rule over the enemy. Adam and Eve had been told to subdue and have dominion over the creatures, but when the creature arrived neither of them obeyed the command of God. Now is the time for male and female to accept the mandate of our Creator, take our place with Christ Jesus, and begin to rule and reign in this life as joint-heirs of the grace of God.

IMPLICATIONS FOR MEN AND WOMEN

As leaders in the church we must examine our paradigms. Are we living as if Christ died in vain? Can we be restored in our relationships with each other through faith in Jesus Christ? If so, we must begin to live with a "pre-fall" mindset. When we see ourselves as redeemed, joint-heirs of the grace of God, we will be in communion with God and one another. Instead of living as Adam and Eve did after their sin, blaming each other and separating from one another, we will walk together with God.

The blame game must come to an end in the church. We see it among women in the form of "male bashing". Among men we see it as "woman blaming". Let us acknowledge our own sin and take responsibility for it before God. Blaming others continues to open the door for the enemy to rule us. We must close the door to the enemy and rule over him.

Strongholds of gender prejudice that have been passed from generation to generation must be addressed by the church. Strongholds are built around our sin nature. The sin nature is anti-God, anti-Christ, anti-Holy Spirit and anti-body of Christ. Our sin nature to be against one another is nailed to the cross of Christ. It is a strong wall of hostility which is demolished by embracing the cross. Paul tells us that the strongholds of our thinking and imaginations must be cast down, if we are to be effective warriors. To keep strongholds in place is to weaken our weapons.

This chapter indicates the struggle of accepting each other's gifts. We must particularly be open to the discerning gift of the Holy Spirit. Men can be helped by hearing a discerning woman. Rather than believing a warning is against you, know it is for your protection. On the other hand, those with discerning gifts must distinguish between suspicion, paranoia and discerning. Intuition or impressions must be taken to God for answers. If you receive no answer or confirmation be quiet and pray. Wait for God to initiate opportunities to share.

One of many times, this gift has operated in my life in regard to my husband and another woman. At first, I thought I may be jealous or suspicious of this woman. I prayed about what I perceived. God answered in a dramatic dream. I knew it was a God dream and asked Him what I should do. He impressed me to wait for a quiet time with my husband and gently share the dream. When I found that moment, my husband responded with gratefulness and affirmation of me. He knew God was warning him for his protection and to save our marriage and ministry.

Essential to victory is the ability to watch and work. The story of Nehemiah is a clear picture of the necessity of watchmen on the wall and workers in the field. The watchmen were to warn the workers when the enemy was encroaching, so they would not be caught off guard. The restoration was completed in record time because each team fulfilled their place. Leaders need to receive the help of those with a watchman anointing.

The gifts and anointing of God are not gender specific. Man or woman can function in any of God's callings. Many women function in a watchman anointing with the discerning of spirits. Sometimes reference is made to mothers as "knowing everything before you know" or "having eyes in all sides of their heads". Women who have a strong intuition are more likely to function in the gift of discerning of spirits. Women working with men who are weak in that area can experience misunderstandings. They may be accused of being negative or critical. Sharing what you perceive to be a warning needs to also include faith in God to overcome.

All gifts and callings are necessary for us to be victorious and advance the purposes of God. Be open to the function of God's gifts through anyone –male or female, bond or free, Jew or Greek. We are all equal in Christ Jesus.

(Endnotes)

1   *Keil and Delitzsch Commentary on the Old Testament: New Updated Edition.* Electronic Database. (Hendrickson Publishers, Inc., 1996).

2   Cunningham, Loren, and David Hamilton. *Why Not Women?.* YWAM Publishing: Seattle, 2000, p. 98.

3   Adam Clarke's Commentary, Electronic Database. Electronic Database. (Biblesoft, Inc., 1996, 2003.)

4   Keil and Delitzsch Commentary on the Old Testament: New Updated Edition.

5   Cunningham and Hamilton. Ibid. p 23.

6   Spencer Aida Bensancon. *Beyond the Curse.* Hendrickson Publishers, 1985. p.35

7   Eldredge, John and Stasi. *Captivating.* Nelson Publishers, 2005, p.85.

8   Scorgie, Glen. *The Journey Back to Eden.* Zondervan, 2005, p. 73.

9   Silvoso, Ed. Women God's *Secret Weapon,* p. 109 from Hebrew Word Pictures, Frank T Seekins, (Phoenix, AZ: Living Word Pictures, p. 1, 72.73)

10 Cunningham and Hamilton. *Why Not Women?* p. 200.

11 Conner, Kevin J. *The Ministry of Women.* KJC Publications: Victoria, Australia, 2003, p. 29.

12 Ibid., p. 30.

13 Grady, Lee. *Ten Lies the Church Tells Women.* Creation House, 2000, p.28.

14 Scorgie. *The Journey Back to Eden.* p. 87.

5

RESTORED TOGETHER

"ALSO FOR ADAM AND HIS WIFE THE LORD GOD
MADE TUNICS OF SKIN, AND CLOTHED THEM"
(GEN. 3:21).

The concept of restoration is not difficult to understand. The root word is *restore* which means simply to return to an original condition. When something is broken, it needs to be restored. Biblically, restoration is the process of God throughout history from the day of the original sin of Adam and Eve to bring humankind back to His original purpose for them. They lost their intimacy with Him, their image of who they were and their unity with each other.

God had a plan to restore them. He gave us the first glimpse of His plan of restoration in the midst of the original sin. Their attempt to cover their sin by some human work would never redeem them. Sin required the shedding of blood for redemption. "For without the shedding of blood, there is no redemption" (Heb. 9:22). Therefore God had to kill an animal to provide a covering for their sin. We refuse God's plan of restoration every time we attempt to be restored through our own efforts, laws and legalistic systems. Until Jesus came, the only means of redemption was by fulfilling the law.

From the beginning, throughout the Old Covenant, God's

people were under the Law. But as Paul proclaimed in Romans 7:24-25, "O wretched man that I am! Who will deliver me from this body of death? I thank God — through Jesus Christ our Lord!" Then in Galatians 3:13-14 he declares to us in the New Covenant: "Christ has redeemed us from the curse of the law, having become a curse for us for it is written, "Cursed is everyone who hangs on a tree", that the blessing of Abraham might come upon the Gentiles in Christ Jesus, that we might receive the promise of the Spirit through faith".

RESTORED TO MATURITY

The ultimate price has been paid for us to live out the mandate of God in the earth. We all come through the same blood – the shed blood of Jesus for our redemption. Kulane Spake refers to Christ as "ERA—Equal Redemption for All."[1] There is no respecter of persons with Jesus. As David Hamilton observes, "Jesus came to set in motion the healing God had promised when Adam and Eve shared the great tragedy of the Garden. He came to end the painful consequences of a broken and sinful world, including the rift between men and women."[2]

Through faith in Jesus Christ any one can be restored to intimacy with God, be conformed to His image and walk in unity with others. We understand being restored to God, but we must choose to live out restoration with ourselves and each other. In so choosing, we recognize that we have been given personal authority by the word of God and the power of the Holy Spirit. It is not an authority given by other human beings. Personal authority comes from God and is released through the word in us and the release of the gifts of the Holy

Spirit given to us by God. Each person is uniquely gifted and called by God for His image to be manifested in their life. When we deny or refuse to allow those gifts to be manifested, we deny the release of the process of restoration. Jesus did not redeem us only to get us to heaven. He redeemed us so we can release His purposes in us in the earth. Every redeemed child of God needs to recognize the giftedness of God in their lives and be willing to steward their gifts for the benefit of others.

Accepting our individual gifts and personal authority, puts us in a place of security so we can accept others' gifts and authority. If I will not face who I am then I will always be threatened by who you are. This issue is a major hindrance to our being restored to unity with one another. Ephesians states clearly that the gifts are given so we can grow up into the fullness of Him (Eph. 4:13). James Robison speaks of this passage. "Through the full operation of the gifts and ministries that God appoints, and operating in the love essential to His own nature, the church will reach a level of maturity and unity that can be measured only in terms of the stature of the fullness of Christ."[3]

Unity of the Body of Christ is a subject of many great books. I simply need to apply the principle to the relationship of male and female. If we will not accept a person's gift or calling because of nationality, gender or social status, we will not know unity. We are one in Christ Jesus! This is easy to talk about as a lofty ideal, but we are called to live it. Therefore, we must begin to recognize each other by gifting and calling rather than by natural preconceptions. When God chooses to use a person without respect to our personal opinion, we should accept the authority and anointing of the gift in them.

An outstanding example of this principle is lived out in

Hispanic Churches in America. Hispanic Christians value one thing over the cultural dynamics and stereotypes of the people. They value the anointing. They value the presence and ministry of the Holy Spirit. President of the National Hispanic Christian Leadership Conference gave this quote in *Ministries Today*; "More important than gender is the testimony of God. Our people will follow whoever is carrying the mantle regardless of gender, stated Sergio Navarrette, superintendent of the southern Pacific Latin district of the Assemblies of God.[4] The article also notes the phenomenal growth of Hispanic churches in the U.S being "co-driven by women".

To limit the release of gifts based on gender, or any other prejudice, is to violate the work of Jesus through us. Jesus' attitude toward women is obvious as we read the gospel accounts. In light of the fact that the Old Covenant law still had an effect on the gender prejudices of Jesus' time. Religious oppression and deprecation of women was still prevalent. Susan Hyatt gives several examples of the social practices of His day. "In the Jerusalem temple, women were limited to one outer portion, the women's court, which was five steps below the court for men. A rabbi regarded it beneath his dignity to speak to a woman in public. Women were kept for childbearing and rearing and were always kept under the strict control of a man."[5]

JESUS RESTORED WOMEN

How amazing that Jesus' value of women violated the traditions of man on many occasions. The most striking example of this is in John 4 where Jesus met the Samaritan woman. Several violations of religious tradition and bias are noted here: 1. He spoke with a woman and was alone with her, 2. She was a Samaritan, 3. She was not living with her husband, even though she had five. Those three characteristics alone were enough to get a man in trouble, but not Jesus. He recognized her as a woman who needed a drink of life. When she recognized who He was, she was changed and became an evangelist to her city. Scripture says she went to tell the men. "And at this point His disciples came, and they marveled that He talked with a woman; yet no one said, "What do You seek?" or, "Why are You talking with her?" The woman then left her water pot, went her way into the city, and said to the men, "Come, see a Man who told me all things that I ever did. Could this be the Christ?" Then they went out of the city and came to Him" (John 4:27-30). Jesus did what no religious leader of the day would do. He ministered to and released a woman to tell the men the good news. She became the first evangelist to reach a city.

Women were a part of the company of Jesus everywhere he went. They offered him assistance and helped support his ministry. Luke 8:1-3 cites several women who were with Him and the disciples. Their financial support of His ministry is noted as well. Jesus refused to accept discrimination against women. Most Jews considered it improper, even obscene, to teach women the Scriptures.[6] Jesus taught and ministered to women publicly. When Mary sat at Jesus' feet, it was a "common expression used to show the formal mentoring relationship between a rabbi and his disciple."[7] Jesus recognized women as worthy of education, even religious instruction.

He accepted women as part of His ministry. They came alongside Him in ministry. Bilezikian points out, "If a disciple is to be defined as a follower, a student and a servant, the women who traveled with

Jesus and the twelve during His itinerant ministry certainly qualified for the designation."[8] When we look at the numerous occasions Jesus ministered to women, we must admit His attitude toward them was contrary to the gender prejudice of the day. We never see Him respond to a woman, even one caught in adultery, in a demeaning way. His heart was full of mercy, compassion and a desire for the restoration of women.

THE NEW COVENANT WOMAN

The sacrifice of Jesus as our Redeemer reconciles us to God and to one another. Under the Old Covenant law, life was lived under the consequences of the fall. "The fundamental difference between the old-covenant people and the new-covenant family is the reversal of the effects of the fall within the latter."[9] In the beginning of the Old Testament the First Lady, Eve, had an encounter with the unholy and was deceived along with man. In the New Testament, the First Lady had an encounter with the Holy Angel and conceived truth and shares the truth with men. The Old Testament First Lady was promised her seed would overcome the enemy. The New Testament First Lady, Mary, conceives the Seed of Victory. Mary, the handmaiden of the Lord, was willing to endure the pain of rejection, violation of traditions, and childbearing to bring forth the Savior. Women warriors are capable of great endurance and perseverance for the SEED in them to bring forth life. In the New Covenant, the enemy now faces the Savior, Redeemer, Deliverer of Humankind. Death will yield to life.

At the death and resurrection of Jesus, we find a company of First Ladies who are the first to experience victory. They encounter holy angels and the truth of victory over death. Truth that overcomes every lie of the deceiver – his power is broken in the resurrection. These women are the first to encounter the truth, and the truth sets them free. We see from the gospels the impact of Jesus' ministry on the women.

From Luke 24:1-12, we make some significant observations. First, women are willing to give courageous acts of worship and devotion. They overcame the greatest fear (even the fear of death) because the perfect love of their Lord compelled them to minister to the body of their Lord. Women express deep love and affection through acts of worship. They will give up their own comforts and desires to express their devotion. God will find women who will come out of hiding and demonstrate their love for Him through acts of obedience.

They are the first to find the barrier of death broken. And they said among themselves, "Who will roll away the stone from the door of the tomb for us?" But when they looked up, they saw that the stone had been rolled away — for it was very large (Mark 16:3, 4). They found the stone rolled away. The Barrier Breaker had broken through every barrier of deception and death! Their concern of removing the stone was answered by the power of the Barrier Breaker! The stone of sin, reproach, oppression and fear was not only rolled away from the tomb, but rolled away for women. Their release came through their desire to minister to the body of their Lord. The new day had come for women to be released.

Though the barrier was broken, an empty tomb caused them much distress. In this distress, they encounter the holy angels, "Do not be afraid, for I know that you seek Jesus who was crucified. He is not here; for He is risen as He said" (Luke 24:6). Glory begins to manifest in their distress. Death from the disobedience in the first garden was now overcome by life in the second garden. Woman may have heard a lie from the evil angel, but now she has heard life from the Holy Angel. The Deceiver is defeated. Women are the first to hear the truth of the Kingdom.

In your distress, you need to remember what He has said to you. Often fulfillment comes in the midst of our distress; we just forget what He said. The promise of resurrection had been spoken, but they forgot the promise in their distress. When they were reminded, indeed they realized they were experiencing the reality of truth. Oh, what glory they were basking in! They had never experienced anything like this moment. Yet, He would not let them sit in the glory. They must obey His orders. Sometimes we want to sit where we are instead of walking to where He is sending us.

These women were told by the angels that He was raised from the dead and were given orders. "And go quickly and tell His disciples that He is risen from the dead, and indeed He is going before you into Galilee; there you will see Him. Behold, I have told you" (Matt. 28:7). As they were going in obedience, Jesus himself meets them to encourage and confirm the orders.

Then Jesus said to them, "Do not be afraid. Go and tell my brothers to go to Galilee; there they will see me" (Matt. 28:10, NIV). Women were the first to be sent with the good news of the gospel. Go tell the apostles and don't be afraid! Imagine, the women were the first to see the resurrected Lord and were sent by the angel and Jesus to go tell the men. No wonder they were told, "Don't be afraid."

Can you imagine having an awesome, glorious experience in the midst of the greatest distress your church has known and being told to go tell the board of elders? You would be scared too. What are the fears we must face if we are going to obey? Fear of rejection – these women had been with these men for years, perhaps they knew them well. "Will they believe us? Will they be angry? They'll say we're crazy." But this fear was overcome with the good news they knew to be true. What encouragement when, as they went, Jesus met them. What confirmation! He affirmed them and encouraged them not to be afraid.

Matthew Henry says regarding this, "The women are sent to tell it to them, and so are made, as it were, the apostles of the apostles. This was an honour put upon them, and a recompense for their constant affectionate adherence to him, at the cross, and in the grave, and a rebuke to the disciples who forsook him."[10] Clearly, these women were the first "witnesses of the resurrection". In Acts, we find this was one designation of the apostles and early Christians (Acts 1:22; 2:32; 4:33). Since the women were witnesses and sent by Jesus to tell the good news, perhaps He was establishing them in a new place of leadership.

The men didn't believe them. At least two of them did go see for themselves. The women had no further responsibility from Jesus. They had done what He said. The reaction to the truth is not your responsibility. Obviously, the women let Jesus take care of the doubt and unbelief of the apostles (Mark 16:14). Neither did they let the rejection of the truth they shared stop them from future obedience. They were in the upper room on the day of Pentecost. Often we take rejection personally when we have obediently given a message. Your obedience to God is your only responsibility not what others think or do with the truth.

The first women to encounter the good news of the risen Lord were the forerunners of the "great host of women" prophesied in Psalm 68:11. The Lord gives the command; The women who proclaim the good tidings are a great host (NASU). When Dr. Yonggi Cho, pastor of the world's largest church in Seoul, Korea was asked, "What's the key to your church?" I tell them again, 'Release your women'..."[11] It is time for women to take the torch and be God's First Ladies to shout the good news. We are not created to spread bad news, gossip or rumor. Our destiny is to shout the victory of our Lord, to proclaim the good news of freedom to those who are oppressed.

GENDERS COMING TOGETHER

In restoring women, Jesus was breaking the old patterns determined by the fall and establishing a "new creation". The new creation Jesus made was breaking all the old laws and restoring humankind to God's original plan from the beginning. Ephesians 2:10 makes it clear, 'For we are God's masterpiece. He has created us anew in Christ Jesus, so that we can do the good things he planned for us long ago' (NLT).

Do we truly believe we have been created anew? We are not just a natural physical creation but a spiritual creation with the Holy Spirit's endowment to accomplish God's mandate in the earth. The Scripture goes on to say that Jesus broke the wall of enmity between the races symbolized in Jew and Gentile, which is a strong wall (Eph. 2:14). There should be no doubt that if the enmity between Jew and Gentile can be reconciled in Jesus then certainly male and female, slave and free can be reconciled. We are one in Christ Jesus. Holy Spirit, help us to believe and live our lives as new creations given to the ministry of reconciliation. "Therefore, if anyone is in Christ, he is a new creation; old things have passed away; behold, all things have become new. Now all things are of God, who has reconciled us to Himself through Jesus Christ, and has given us the ministry of reconciliation," (2 Cor. 5:17-18). Barnes note on this passage states:

> It means, evidently, that there is a change produced in the renewed heart of man that is equivalent to the act of creation, and that bears a strong resemblance to it-a change, so to speak, as if the man was made over again, and had become new...In regard to all, it is also true that old things pass away. Their former prejudices, opinions, habits, attachments pass away. Their supreme love of self passes away. Their love of sins passes away.[12]

To believe we are a new creation means we will not continue to live the old life of pride and prejudice with regard to others. We will accept every believer as one recreated in Jesus to fulfill God's mandate for their life. We offer equal opportunity for a believing Jew to serve according to his gift. If a "slave" is born again, we do not deny them the opportunity to serve. But saved women are often denied opportunities to function in their gifts.

We will come together as male and female to rule in this life. God's original plan for mankind would only be fulfilled by the coming of the Redeemer. He knew the treatment of women in His day would not allow them to fulfill their mandate from the beginning. Part of the original mandate to them was to take dominion over the creation. He gave them responsibilities that required them to make decisions, plan and use authority. They were created to be leaders. We lost a lot in the fall, most importantly our relationship and fellowship with God. We also lost our ability to fulfill the mandate to rule. Jesus came to restore us to a position of authority in the earth. Myles Munroe says, "You were born to lead, but you must become a leader. Every human being was endowed by the Creator with leadership potential in a specific area of gifting. The human spirit is designed to manage and control its world and it functions best when creating an environment conducive to this pursuit."[13]

Jesus was not only about restoring individuals to God, but also restoring humankind to fulfill God's plan from the beginning. Restoring women was essential to that because He told Adam from the beginning, "It was not good for him to be alone". Male and female must not be isolated from each other, but reconciled and restored to His purposes for them. Glen Scorgie sums up Jesus' ministry to women. "Jesus, the Spirit-filled liberator and supreme revealer of God's will and ways, inaugurated a new attitude toward women and established patterns of respect toward them that were unprecedented in his time. He indicated in this way the direction the Spirit was headed in the redemptive task of restoring the original pattern of equality, freedom and mutuality in gender relations."[14]

If Jesus could accept women in His ministry, why shouldn't male leaders today accept them as equal laborers? In the words of Kevin Conner, "Both men and women are called to function together in Divine order, in love and harmony as members of the Body of Christ, under Christ's headship."[15]

IMPLICATIONS FOR MEN AND WOMEN

What does it mean in real life to live out the restoration of God? Let us consider a few possible scenarios.

Perhaps you are the "leader" of a team trying to make strategic plans. One of the team members receives a "word of wisdom" that would be a precise strategic plan. As "leader" would you see this as the gift it is or as the "member" trying to tell you what to do? I have observed on many occasions where the leader has perceived the member trying to tell them what to do. This seems often the case if the member is a woman and the leader is a man. If a leader can not accept wisdom from another man, they have a deep personal issue; but, if it is only from women they can not receive, they have a "woman" issue. Likewise, women leaders can have a "man" issue because they perceive men as always trying to tell them what to do.

Another common scenario for Pentecostal/Charismatic people relates to corporate worship. We enjoy freedom to worship God and experience His manifest presence. We call it the anointing or manifested glory. I believe in protocol, an established order of releasing the gifts of God in the corporate worship time. As restored people, we should be able to accept the anointing flowing from one to another. Yet, we often see leaders who are greatly annoyed if the anointing on one person surpasses their anointing at the moment. God does not desire the Spirit to be quenched or leadership to be usurped.

In either scenario, we see the common issue of pride that we all must deal with in our lives. To come to unity with each other, we will have to die to OUR agendas, opinions and prejudices. Male or female, leader or member can be used of God according to the measure of faith given them. It is not by any merit of our own that we have any authority; it is the gift of God in us.

Another implication of living as restored people is releasing positional authority by recognizing personal authority. Suppose you are gifted by God in a particular gift (personal authority) but you have no place to function in that gift (positional authority). Proverbs says that your gift will make room for you (Proverbs 18:16). Positional authority is basically confirmed and granted by the Body of Christ in a local church or ministry. So if the authority or gifting in you is not confirmed by others, you are without positional authority and that is frustrating to you. By the same token, when the body refuses to recognize a person's gifting, they are depriving the Body of that authority and anointing. The authority connection is missing. When your personal authority and positional authority come together, you realize a greater release of the image of God in you.

The Body of Christ often misses one or the other. We give someone positional authority without the personal authority to match it. For example, a gifted teacher is asked to serve in a position not comparable to their gift. Even worse is the common practice in many ministries where the position is determined by the vote of the people. The vote seldom has anything to do with the gifting or personal authority one walks in. When we can spiritually discern the Body and the gifting of God in each one, we can get positioned to fulfill the mandate of God to rule in the earth.

(Endnotes)
1   Spake, Kulane.*From Enmity to Equality*. Workforce Press, Suwanee, GA, p. 25
2   Cunningham, Loren, and David Hamilton. *Why Not Women?* YWAM Publishing: Seattle, 2000, p. 111.
3   Hayford, Jack. *Spirit - Filled Life Bible*. General Editor: Nelson Publishers, 1991, p. 2017.
4   (Ministries Today, July/August 2006, Death of Machismo, by Sam Rodriguez, president of the National Hispanic Christian Leadership Conference. p.48)
5   Hyatt, Susan. *In the Spirit We Are Equal*. Hyatt Press, Dallas, TX, 1998, p. 14.
6   Cunningham and Hamilton. *Why Not Women?* p. 119.
7   Ibid., 121.
8   Bilezikian, Gilbert. *Beyond Sex Roles,* Baker Book House, 1985. p. 96.
9   Ibid., p. 79.
10   *Matthew Henry's Commentary on the Whole Bible: New Modern Edition*. Electronic Database. (Hendrickson Publishers, Inc., 1991).
11   Cunningham and David. *Why Not Women?* p. 68.
12   Barnes' Notes. Electronic Database. (Biblesoft, Inc., 1997, 2003).
13   Munroe, Dr. Myles. *The Spirit of Leadership*. Whitaker House, 2005, p. 48.
14   Scorgie, Glen. *The Journey Back to Eden*. Zondervan, 2005, p. 127.
15   Conner, Kevin J. *The Ministry of Women*. KJC Publications: Victoria, Australia, 2003, p. 72.

6

LEADING TOGETHER

"BUT TO EACH ONE OF US GRACE WAS GIVEN ACCORDING
TO THE MEASURE OF CHRIST'S GIFT"
(EPH. 4:7, NIV).

The grace of God is in many ways incomprehensible. How God, the Infinite, All Wise One, can take finite, unwise humans and use them for His glory is a great mystery. The marvel is that He has given "each one" of us a measure of grace gifting. Those gifts are not of our choosing but at His divine discretion. Teaching on the discovery and use of your gifts has been prevalent in recent years, yet we have a tendency to limit the use of the gifts according to some traditional doctrine. This is particularly true with regard to women using their gifts.

My husband was given an assignment in the 70's to teach a college course on marriage and the family. He decided the best way to teach it was as husband and wife. This put us on a fast course to study the Christian literature available. We discovered most of it emphasized the wife's role of submission and lesser emphasis on the husband's role of sacrifice. Seldom was there any discussion of "mutual submission" in marriage as given in Ephesians 5:21. After forty years of marriage, we have come to understand Christ is the head of our home and we both submit to Him and one another.

Personally my biggest question in those days was, "Why would God call me to teach and then say I couldn't teach?" I knew I was called by God for ministry to the Body of Christ. Not being able to find fulfillment in the church with my call, I chose the professional road in public schools. Then, quite abruptly, one year the Holy Spirit spoke to me to resign my position and 'trust Him as He had a school for me'. After much prayer with my husband, we knew it was His direction, even though, financially it made no sense. To say the least, those were adventurous years of faith and paradigm shifting. God's school was one of prayer, study and practice. I came to understand His gifts in my life were not limited by Him.

Scripture is clear that all the gifts in Roman 12, 1 Corinthians 12 and Ephesians 4 are given by God without respect of persons. We are one Body and each has his God-given part to fulfill. As Paul states, "We then, as workers together with Him also plead with you not to receive the grace of God in vain" (2 Corinthians 6:1). All the gifts are grace gifts, and we frustrate the grace of God by not exercising them. As workers together with Him we acknowledge our part as a result of His grace. He chose us and destined us for His purposes. We must never forget we are accountable to God. Every person will answer to God for His stewardship of the grace of God given them. What have you done with the gifts God has given you? We answer for ourselves to God alone.

GIFTED LEADERSHIP: MAN AND WOMAN

Understanding that God has gifted women, as well as men, we desire to understand how the unique characteristics and gifts of each can work together. Some will say we have been working together and that is true, but the issue at hand is leadership. With a plethora of leadership books available and read by multitudes, we should know leadership. Dr. Myles Munroe sums up some key issues regarding leadership, "There are many who confuse the *position* of leadership with the *dis-position* of true leadership (emphasis added). Others have confused leadership with the ability to control others through manipulation of their emotions, and playing on their fears and needs. But true leadership is a product of inspiration, not manipulation. True leadership is the discovery of one's purpose and assignment for life, and the inherent gifts and abilities that come with that assignment, and the commitment to serve that gift to the world to improve the lives of many. True leadership is not measured by how many people serve you but by how many people you serve."[1] We must begin to recognize leadership potential in any person and allow their potential to be developed and deployed in the church – even when it is a woman. Kevin J. Conner authored *The Ministry of Women* in 1984 with several reprints, but in 2003 he published the enlarged and expanded edition. He made a major shift in this most recent edition stating, "After much more study of the role, function and ministry of women, there is really nothing that a woman cannot do any more or less than a man. The key is: IF God calls, equips and anoints a man or a woman to do something, then that is His grace."[2]

Gretchen Hull believes, "Men will bring a male perspective and women a female perspective. When both minister together –in line with their mutual creation in the image of God and in fulfillment of Jesus' prayer in John 17:20-23 – they will begin to mirror the unity, equality, harmony, and cooperation of the Godhead."[3] Dr. J. Robert Clinton, professor of Leadership at Fuller Theological Seminary and an adjunct professor at Southwestern Christian University, has researched leadership all his professional life. Dr. Clinton has come from a very conservative position to what many would call a rather liberal one. His present position has come as the result of much study and observation within the academic community. He has not overlooked the issue of female leadership and states his present position as "Interdependent Ministry—joint influence of male and female is needed to bring balance and needed components of leadership ministry." He goes on to state five supportive explanations:

1. Males bring certain components to leadership that females don't.
2. Females bring certain components to leadership that males don't.
3. Both are needed in an overall situation. An extension of the interdependent body ethic to leadership.
4. Either could have top leadership depending on giftedness and experience.
5. Women and men can operate positionally.[4]

My own journey has provided five paradigm shifts in the area of gender balanced leadership. My first paradigm of women in leadership was watching my own grandmother and her daughter minister and pastor churches. I was raised in a classical Pentecostal tradition, which held a theological position that women could be ordained in ministry. In practice, women were given small churches that could not salary a full time pastor. I have lived out the second paradigm of a woman being in ministry with her husband. I have served with my husband as teacher and pastor. In recent years, married couples serving together as pastors have been common. Women leading itinerant ministries, while their husbands assist them, are not an uncommon practice. The third paradigm shift is related to single women who were ordained as missionaries. They could serve on foreign soil without a husband. As single women called to foreign mission work they were able to function as teachers, pastors or leaders outside the U.S. The fourth paradigm shift came more recently in accepting God's sovereign giftedness in men and women as the basis of ministry regardless of gender. The practice of this paradigm still has some inequalities when it comes to fulfilling leadership roles. For example, men are often preferred over a woman who is equally qualified for a position men have traditionally held. Women may serve on boards but not as chairperson. The matter of financial distribution has also been observed in this inequality. Women may hold the same position or even replace a man in a position but are paid less salary. The fifth paradigm is that of men and women serving equally to fulfill God's mandate before the fall in the Garden of Eden. The church has made significant progress in these paradigm shifts, and we are all at various stages. Each shift moves us closer toward God's original intent for humankind. The original intent of the Creator was for male and female to co-labor together in His purposes for them to rule the earth.

CO-LABORERS

We must develop in our relationship with each other to a place of mutual respect so we can co-labor together in leadership. It is not a matter of the men doing their thing and allowing the women to do their thing. We know we need leadership that is balanced in its gift mix. No one gift will be able to advance the Kingdom of God and neither will just one gender be able to take dominion over the earth.

I do not believe that women can accomplish God's destiny for them without men, but neither can men fulfill God's commission without women. God said, "It is not good that man should be alone." So He created another human to complement him in fulfilling their God given assignment. Therefore men and women are needed by each other. God's desire is to see a unity of the genders with His heart to fulfill His purposes in the earth.

We must consider the restoration of equality as part of the redemptive work of Christ as stated in Galatians 3:28. When we examine this verse in light of its context, we see the entire chapter is dealing with the old laws as opposed to the new and living way of faith.

"Wherefore the law was our schoolmaster to bring us unto Christ, that we might be justified by faith. But after that faith is come, we are no longer under a schoolmaster. For ye are all the children of God by faith in Christ Jesus. For as many of you as have been baptized into Christ have put on Christ. There is neither Jew nor Greek, there is neither bond nor free, there is neither male nor female: for ye are all one in Christ Jesus." (Galatians 3:24-28, KJV)

Paul is very clear and specific regarding who is free in Christ. There can be no discrimination of nationality, social class or gender. What a disgrace that the Body of Christ has not lived that reality through the centuries. Bitter battles have been fought over those discriminations. God desired from the beginning for all people to be reconciled to Him and each other through faith in Jesus. We have made some progress in each of those areas, but we must continue to overcome our prejudices. May we apply the biblical principle of grace and faith to our relationships as male and female.

Paul, himself, ministered as a single man but acknowledged the assistance of several women. In Romans 16 he lists ten women by name who labored with him in ministry. Junia is noted as an apostle. "Greet Andronicus and Junia, my countrymen and my fellow prisoners, who are of note among the apostles, who also were in Christ before me" (Rom 16:7). Rena Pederson, author of *The Lost Apostle*, has done extensive research on the life of Junia as a female apostle.

We are now living in a world that expects more grace and compassion in the church than we have demonstrated in times past. Diane Passno, Executive Vice President of *Focus on the Family* rehearses the history of the church's missed opportunity. "The Church has always played such a strong role in our culture. How did feminists supersede that role and the traditional teaching of the Church in their quests for "rights"? It is my feeling that they would never have won the minds and loyalty of women if the Church had addressed women's concerns from the start. Feminism could so easily have been a Christian movement within the structure of the Church because it had everything to do with human dignity. Why wasn't it? Was male leadership so entrenched in denominations that it couldn't see or understand the issues?"

She goes on to recount the efforts of Frances Willard and the Women's Christian Temperance Union and Susan Anthony with the women's suffrage movement such as Clara Barton and the American Red Cross and Rosa Parks and her stance for racial equality.

> The organized Church had every conceivable reason to be involved in these areas as well, but was not. Because of confusion over the role of women scripturally in marriage as well as in the workplace, the pulpit was not in sync with the reality of women's lives...their concerns, their areas of giftedness, their ability to contribute to the Church and society in ways other than teaching Sunday School.[5]

My heart cries out for the church to redeem the time. We must rise up and come together as one – male and female – to fulfill God's mandate to us. For us to be fully restored to God's original intent to rule creation, we must acknowledge the mandate is given to both – male and female.

SERVANT LEADERSHIP FOR ALL

What is our concept of leadership? Are leaders those who have rule over others? Are they slave masters? Are they the ones who make all the decisions? Though many definitions of leadership have been given by great authors, the most important definition to followers of Christ is Christ's own definition. The disciples were rather concerned about their greatness or positions in His kingdom. His answer to their concerns was not what they expected. "You know that the rulers of the Gentiles lord it over them, and those who are great exercise authority over them. Yet it shall not be so among you; but whoever desires to become great among you, let him be your servant. And whoever desires to be first among you, let him be your slave—just as the Son of Man did not come to be served, but to serve and to give His life a ransom for many" (Matt. 20:25-28).

Should this not be our basis for determining leaders among us? It is commonly referred to as "servant leadership", but how often is it practiced? Until we come to the cross of dying to our own desires for power and position, we will continue to compete and control. Jesus model of leadership is the most successful model ever lived. He was selfless and totally submitted to the will of His Father. Has He called each of us to anything less?

Related to our concept of leadership is our desire for control. George Barna cites ten reasons we are reluctant to embrace a team leadership model. His second reason is the issue of control. "Giving up control is a major issue for many individuals and remains a major obstacle for tens of thousands of American churches…The result is that creativity is stifled and decisions are limited by the intelligence, sensitivity and the experience of the dictator…Trying to serve within an environment in which one individual is controlling and domineering becomes oppressive."[6]

Interestingly, the original sin of Adam and Eve included a desire for control of their lives. They yielded to the temptation to be wise as God (Gen. 3:5-6). We continue to struggle with the same temptation. But God, through Jesus has made a way of escape for us— the cross. We died with Him – our flesh is crucified – desire for power, glory; pride and selfishness and all that is not of Him. The way of the cross is the only means to break the barrier of division (Eph. 2:14-16). We would rather fight for our rights to be in control than embrace the cross. When in truth we have no rights but to be children of God. To embrace the cross requires humility. Jesus humbled himself through obedience even to the death of the cross (Phil. 2:8). Our refusal to humble ourselves in obedience to God is the root of our divisions.

GENDER DIVIDED

Pride is what keeps us separated and deceived. We believe we are right in denying each other the freedom to follow Christ as He leads us. Our prejudices are justified by our pride. "Prejudice is not a primary sin; it's a secondary sin. It derives from a basic sense of pride. Prejudice arises from the soils of fear and ignorance, though ironically, prejudice is learned."[7] Jesus never taught or practiced any prejudice. He accepted all persons and treated them with respect and honor. When we embrace the cross by facing our fears and crucifying our pride, we will be able to embrace each other.

Shortly after my husband and I started dating in Bible College, Garnet tested me. At the tender age of 19, I was clueless to his test. He asked me to the "big event" of the year nearly a month in advance. I was thrilled and then he said, "You can not tell anyone I've asked you." "Why?" was my reply. "Because it is off if you do." End of conversation. What a bummer! I lived in a dorm where every girl was waiting to be asked (in the 60's boys asked girls for dates). The event required a formal dress which I did not possess. A week before the event, he said that I could ask my friend if I could borrow one of her many dresses. The date was delightful, but I was still clueless to the test and so were my friends. Finally, he shared with me his purpose for his test. "I had to know I could trust you," he said. Since then we have discussed this issue of men trusting women many times. He agrees it is generally a learned prejudice and fear. His prior relationships with women proved to him that women talk too much and can not be trusted. The issue is not how we come by our fears and prejudices, but are we determined to overcome them.

The other side of this coin was my prejudice that "men don't listen". I have discovered some reasons they don't listen. Sometimes what we have to say is not pertinent to their concerns. Furthermore, we need to discern the right time to talk. As women we have learned it is best to wait until our opinion is asked when meeting with male leaders. We discern their concerns and try to relate to those issues. Women are amazed when men actually ask for their opinion or their concerns.

A friend, who is an associate producer of an upcoming movie, shared a unique experience with me. The production team includes intercessors (mostly women). The producer (a man) wanted to meet with them. After sharing together he said to the intercessor's leader, "I ask you to come to me anytime you perceive I am manifesting pride or getting off course in any way." What an unusual man! He actually trusted her to confront him. Was he submitting to a woman? This man obviously recognized the gift of God in a woman and knew he needed her help in this assignment. He honored her for what he saw in her. To learn to honor one another without bias is essential if we are to lead together.

A LIFE SUBMITTED

Romans 12 lists the gifts of the Body of Christ as well as the command from Paul to honor and prefer one another. Honoring one another is required by all members of the church, including leaders. Leaders must honor those they serve, not just the members honoring the leader. At times, the gift of leading will need to honor or yield to the gift of helps or the gift of mercy. When a leader gets so focused on the task that the needs of people are being neglected, the gift of mercy or helps will begin to speak to the needs of the people. A leader must recognize that the position of leadership does not come with all the gifts. Every leader, male or female, needs other leaders with different gifts to help them lead.

Being Spirit led includes submission of all members to the Spirit of God first and foremost. Christ is the head of His Church, and we do well to honor Him as the Head by submitting our own ideas to Him. We can not be so naive to believe that we are submitting to Christ when we will not submit to one another. No one is ever exempt from submission to authority. We live under authority wherever we are. When I choose to go in a business establishment, I submit myself to that authority. If they ask me to leave – I leave. I operate by their established policies while I am there. You may be the president of the largest corporation, but when you are in another place of business you are in submission to them. The point is we are all subject to delegated authority. Submission is not a gender biased principle. Men and women must live in submission to authority and honor all people. In the truest sense of honor only God deserves honor; therefore, what I honor in another person is the God potential in them. Even non-believers deserve honor because they are the creation of God. For me to refuse you honor is to deny or not be willing to recognize the grace of God in your life. We honor Christ in each of us – both male and female.

Our world today needs male and female leadership. The old models of leading will not impact this generation. This generation has been raised with a global awareness and accessibility to information that allows them to do their own research for answers. They have raised themselves by taking responsibility for their own lives very early as latch key kids. On the other hand, they have been pampered and encouraged to be all they want to be. They are in need of both nurture and discipline. In the church all babes in Christ need to be fathered and mothered in the gospel. "There is nothing unbiblical about women being mothers and men being fathers in the church (1 Tim. 5:1-2). These terms refer to church leaders…It is not a new thought that the people of God need to be fathered and mothered."[8] As we accept the unique contribution of men and women together in leadership, we will be representing the gospel in a more functional way and thereby helping to correct the dysfunctionality of our society.

Another reason we need to be leaders together is to realize the healing of the land. When Adam and Eve disobeyed, God cursed the land (Gen. 3:17). When men and women are restored and reconciled to each other, they have authority to rule over the land and reverse the curse. Our world is searching for any means to see the earth preserved and to become productive. The redemption, creation groans for, can be realized as the redeemed begin to obey God's original mandate. The mandate to rule the earth is given to both, male and female. The healing of the land is dependent on men and women exercising their joint authority.

IMPLICATIONS FOR MEN AND WOMEN

We must acknowledge pride as the root issue of all our prejudices. I prejudge you according to my flesh and that is not being led by the Spirit. The antithesis of honor is pride. Prejudice is a manifestation of pride and is dishonoring of others. We must seek to demonstrate honor toward both genders in the world.

My experience in the church world has led me to the cross on numerous occasions, nearly always related to my pride. At times it was necessary to confess my attitudes of "superiority", at other times my attitudes of "inferiority" – both rooted in pride. When accused of being "too strong" or "trying to tell others what to do", my pride would rise up and say "no, you are falsely accusing me." At other times my pride would convince me that I did not have anything to contribute – a subtle manifestation of the monster. The truth is I am who I am in Christ and my obedience to love as He loves must be my highest goal. The subtleties of pride must not cause me to disobey Him or move beyond who He has called me to be.

In my research for this book I found few books on "gender balanced leadership", but there are many books on leadership. Researcher, George Barna says,

> "In the past decade there have been more than 4,000 new books written about leadership. Most of them discuss the indispensable skills needed to become king of the hill; few of them downplay the importance of personal superiority in favor of serving within a team context…leadership works best when it is provided by teams of gifted leaders serving together in pursuit of a clear and compelling vision."[9]

To develop team leadership means that we will be open to a diversity of ideas and the creativity of each other's gifts. We would not think of having a leadership team for a multi-cultural church without a representative of the cultures on the team. Yet, we have not had equal representation for women on leadership teams in churches that were at least fifty percent women. Conduct an honest analysis of the diversity of each ministry or leadership team in your church.

Is it possible that women bring a different perspective to leading than men? I believe God created male and female unique, not just in the physical, sexual uniqueness, but unique in our DNA. The scientific world continues to research that possibility.[10] Research and discussion of male/female differences will continue. What we must do is seek to understand one another's unique perspective without prejudging or stereotyping one another.

Giving equal opportunity for service to men and women by releasing them to function in the gifts regardless of gender is the most serious implication for men and women in the church. We must value one another in light of Christ's redemptive work in our lives. Ask the Holy Spirit to deal with our heart issues of prejudice, so His grace can be released through our lives. God will work through those who yield to Him for His original mandate to be fulfilled.

(Endnotes)
1   (Myles Munroe, Ministries Today, March/April 2006 Strang Communications, FL , "The Power of Influence", p37-39)
2   Conner Kevin J. The Ministry of Women. SRM Production Services Sdn Bhd, Malaysia, 2003, p. i
3   Hull, Gretchen. *Equal to Serve.* Baker Book House, MI, 1998, p. 226
4   Clinton, Dr. J Robert. *Gender and Leadership.* Barnabas Publishers, Altadena, CA.,1995, p. 17.
5   Passno, Diane. *Feminism; Mystique or Mistake?* Tyndale House: IL, 2000, p. 18-19.
6   Barna, George. *Building Effective Leadership Teams.* Issachar Resources: Ventura, CA, 2001, p. 55.
7   Sumner, Sarah. *Men and Women in the Church.* InterVarsity Press, IL, 2003, p. 76.
8   Ibid., p. 322.
9   Barna, Ibid., p. 12.
10 Grenz, Stanley. *Women in the Church.* InterVarsity Press, IL, 1995, p. 159.

7

REAPING TOGETHER

"I AM IN THEM AND YOU ARE IN ME.
MAY THEY EXPERIENCE SUCH PERFECT UNITY
THAT THE WORLD WILL KNOW THAT
YOU SENT ME AND THAT YOU LOVE
THEM AS MUCH AS YOU LOVE ME"
(JOHN 17:23, NLT).

Our desire for the world to know the love of Jesus should compel us to embrace the unity Jesus prayed for in this verse. Have you considered gender unity for the sake of the gospel being lived out? If men and women can not live in unity within the church, how can we reach a harvest which suffers from gender abuse? Everyday our news media has to report all types of violence and abuse of the opposite sex, particularly abuse of women. As the church, we must be able to show them a better way – a life of love and peace through Jesus Christ. "The topic of unity among brothers and sisters in the Body is one of the greatest battles the Church must face. Because God's design was for men and women to serve side-by-side, Satan fights to maintain the hierarchy that place men over women. However, when the Church recaptures God's original intent, the unity will result in a great harvest of souls throughout the earth."[1] Most of us would agree that an increase in anointing and blessing would help us reap the harvest. The Psalmist declared that *unity* releases anointing and the Lord's blessing (Ps. 133). Yet, we will hold onto our prejudices that keep us apart, rather than joining together and receiving an increase in anointing and blessing.

BATTLE OF THE AGES

In addition to a lack of unity, a major sinister enemy to harvest is the anti-Christ spirit in the earth. This spirit is anti-against anything and everything Christ is for. It is first and foremost anti-harvest of believers in Jesus Christ. Whatever can be said or done to block people from knowing Jesus is its primary objective. The Church has been in this battle forever.

Historically, we can see various breakthroughs in the battle for souls at several fronts. A theological breakthrough came with the revelation of "justification by faith". What a major upheaval that revelation brought to the body of Christ. The anti-Christ spirit held people in bondage to works and penance for centuries. The truth that you could be saved by grace through faith in Christ alone resulted in a great harvest.

In more recent times, we have seen cultural breakthroughs. These relate to Jesus Christ giving His life for all mankind. It is His will that none should perish and that all ethnos have an opportunity to hear the good news (Matt. 24:14). The church has said, "Whosoever will, come," but has often closed the door to some. Paul identifies three cultures of society which we have struggled to breakthrough. In Galatians 3:28, he declares the gospel is for every nationality, both genders and every class. This passage pinpoints cultural biases that have limited the Church in receiving harvest. God will not exclude anyone or any group from the opportunity to serve Him. Paradigms of exclusiveness block us from receiving people God desires to be saved. Our mindsets are slow to change.

Progress with the cultural barrier of ethnicity has taken years. In the church, we have opened our doors and hearts to let other nationalities in, but have we limited their service? Do our preconceived ideas of another nationality cause us to limit their value? The apostle Paul declares we are one in Christ – no discrimination because of ethnicity. When we allow all nations to be actively involved in service, we open the door for all nations to come to Jesus.

Similarly, we can apply the same principle to the two other barriers in the passage—gender and class. When both genders are represented in service and leadership, it says to men and women, you are valued by us and God. There is no discrimination of gender in Christ. When we are open to receive all classes – rich and poor, my club and your club – we will see a harvest that is representative of our world. Jesus never discriminated because of social status. "Jesus' followers were a preview of the church – male and female, rich and poor, professional and working class, the right and the left—a motley crew who, without changed hearts, could never come together."[2] We must become the church with changed hearts to reap the harvest in this day.

MANDATE OF ALL

We have two mandates to reap a harvest. In the beginning God mandated mankind – male and female – to be fruitful and multiply. The second is the last command of Jesus known as the Great Commission – go ye into all the world. These two mandates are given to all to reach all. It will take all nationalities, all social strata and both genders working together to reap the harvest. Now is the time to overcome the barriers and come together for the sake of the Kingdom of God.

We believe we are facing the opportunity for the greatest harvest in history. The world that needs to see the love of Christ is more female than male. According to the U.S. Census Bureau, Census 2000 Summary File 3, 51 percent of the total population was female. Fifty-eight percent of women 16 and older were in the labor force. Women have found a place of respect for their gifts and abilities in the corporate and political world as leaders, but the church wants to see them converted without allowing them equal opportunity for service. Will we neglect the great harvest of women by refusing to allow women to serve once they are converted?

Our attitudes toward the harvest field will determine how effective we are in reaping. Sarah Sumner shares an encounter with a secular woman. The woman assumed Sarah cared about the church's uncaring attitude of women like her. "She assumed that I cared because I was a woman who had served full-time on the evangelism staff at a famous, seeker-targeted mega-church. Unfortunately, she was dead wrong. I didn't feel burdened for "those women." It had never occurred to me to proclaim the gospel to secular feminists."[3] This encounter brought Sarah to a place of repentance.

If we are serious about harvest, then we must begin to convey to the harvest an attitude of grace and love for them. There is a harvest of women today who are educated, professional and successful in the marketplace. They are accustomed to being honored for their gifts and abilities. Sarah's friend said to her in one encounter, "I meet so many women who refuse to go to church because women in society are more respected as leaders in the world than as participants in the Christian community."[4] It is sad to say this is more common than we want to admit. We know we must deal with our attitudes regarding nationalities and social class to reap a harvest in those areas. Likewise, we must come to a place of repentance and reconciliation regarding our gender prejudices to reap a harvest among women.

Carolyn James makes this observation in her book, *Lost Women of the Bible*; "A whole wave of talented women who are valued and sought out in the workplace for their training, expertise, and leadership skills are walking away from the church because it seems so uninviting to them. Tragically, the message they're picking up is that the church will clip their wings and has nothing hopeful to offer them."[5] The world today offers more opportunities for women leaders than the church offers them. The 2006 primary elections in my state included women running in most races and winning them. Being a woman running for state office was not an issue. The church must not allow gender to be a limitation for function in the church. "Multiplied thousands of women today are alive in Jesus but still tied up by the burial shroud of human tradition—tradition that says they are second-class citizens-and cultural ideas that tell them they cannot carryout out the highest callings of God's kingdom."[6]

Women must deal with their attitudes toward men as well. Many men refuse to attend church because they believe it is a woman's world. There are historical and sociological issues that figure into the reality that the church has been a woman's world, even though in most cases men held the leadership positions. Women are not called to take over or make the church a woman's club. Being sensitive to the needs and preferences of both genders is essential for creating gender balanced teams. Carolyn James further states, "According to the biblical record, the history of men and women working together is longer than men working with men or women working with women… The clear message of the Bible is that God intended for men and women to work together."[7] I am suggesting that until we deal with present attitudes regarding each other, we will not move forward in reaching either gender. This male-female harvest will be reaped as men and women work together in the fields.

GENDERS LIVING FREE

To be effective in the harvest fields, we need a fresh outpouring of the Holy Spirit on all flesh. When Joel prophesied the outpouring of the Spirit he included every facet of society, including men and women. In Acts 2, we read of the beginning of the fulfillment of that prophecy on all flesh – men and women, various ethnic groups and social classes. The church went forth empowered by the Holy Spirit to fulfill the command of Christ. We will do the same as we receive a fresh outpouring of His Spirit. Every outpouring of the Spirit in history has released men and women into harvest.

The Welsh revival of the early 1900's was sparked by women's prayer meetings in a time when women were prohibited expression in the church. In the 1950's, the Hebrides Islands of Scotland experienced a great revival. Duncan Campbell was a leader in that revival with females as colleagues which God used mightily. The Azusa Street Revival board of directors "consisted of five men and seven women".[8]

Hyatt goes on to state, "Authority was not determined by gender, but by the God-ordained expression of the Holy Spirit through the individual person."[9] Women were released in ministry as a result of the Holy Spirit's work in their lives. We must continue to recognize the sovereignty of the Holy Spirit to call whom He wills. He knows who He needs to use to draw people to Jesus. As Jesus said, "The harvest is plentiful but the workers are few. Ask the Lord of the harvest, therefore, to send out workers into his harvest field" (Matt. 9:36-38, NIV). Shall we eliminate half of the workers because God created them female? Jesus never limited the women in fact at His resurrection He mandated them to be His messengers (John 20:17-18).

The harvest is before us as Jesus said after the conversion of the Samaritan woman, "Do you not say, 'There are still four months and then comes the harvest'? Behold, I say to you, lift up your eyes and look at the fields, for they are already white for harvest" (John 4:35)! The disciples were having difficulty with the conversion of a Samaritan woman, a strategic part of the harvest. Are we not able to see because our eyes have been blinded by our own preconceived ideas about Jesus and the harvest? The Bible speaks often of our ability to hear, but not understand and our ability to see, but not perceive. (Mark 4:12, 8:17, Is. 6:9). The inability to understand and perceive is related to the condition of our hearts. Hebrews 3 makes it clear that hardened hearts do not hear, and they fail to act in obedience. Perhaps we need a heart examination by the Holy Spirit to free our hearts to hear and understand the mandate of God to join together as mankind in the earth and reap a harvest of men and women.

IMPLICATIONS FOR MEN AND WOMEN

Renewing a passion for Jesus and compassion for people is the most crucial implication for both men and women in the church. Have we lost our first love? Do we care enough for the harvest to change our attitudes and modus operando? We must take seriously the creation mandate of God and the great commission of Jesus. We are created to rule over the enemy and reap a harvest of souls in the world. Our attitudes toward people will determine our effectiveness in fulfilling our mandates.

As we cry out to God for a renewing of our minds and rending of our hearts, we will be conformed to His image. We will *be* witnesses of His love in the world. Our lives will demonstrate the love and power of God to all.

(Endnotes)
1   Seagraves, Chad and Leslie Neal. *Fishers of People! Cast the Net of the Kingdom!* (Empowering Women and Men to Use Their Gifts Together in Advancing the Gospel, Lausanne Occasional Paper No. 53, Lausanne Committee for World Evangelization, 2005)
2   James, Carolyn Custis. *Lost Women of the Bible.* Zondervan: Grand Rapids, MI, 2005, p.191.
3   Sumner, Sarah. *Men and Women in the Church.* InterVarsity Press, IL. 2003, p. 71.
4   Sumner.Ibid.., p 71.
5   James. *Lost Women of the Bible.* p. 17.
6   Cunningham, Loren, and David Hamilton. *Why Not Women?* YWAM Publishing: Seattle, 2000, p. 27.
7   James. *Lost Women of the Bible.* p. 37.
8   Hyatt, Susan and Fred T. Corum qtd. *Like A Fire: A Reprint of the Old Azusa Street Papers.* Hyatt Press, TX, 1981, p. 202.
9   Ibid., p. 206.

NOTES

NOTES

NOTES

Notes